A Taste of Dreams

Josceline Dimbleby is the author of *Party Pieces,* the *Book of Puddings, Desserts and Savouries* and a series of cookery books for Sainsbury's. She has contributed to a number of newspapers and magazines and has appeared on both television and radio.

The author's childhood, spent amidst the exotic aromas and flavours of the Middle East and South America has developed her tastes for spices and herbs. In this collection of unique recipes she uses these ingredients adventurously, and her aim is to stimulate the reader to have ideas of her own. The result is a mouthwatering selection of dishes ranging from piquant oriental delights to nostalgic English nursery food tailor-made to satisfy simple and exotic tastes alike!

JOSCELINE DIMBLEBY
A Taste of Dreams

Illustrations by Peggy Chapman

 SPHERE BOOKS LIMITED
30/32 Gray's Inn Road, London WC1X 8JL

To David for always making me feel my food is best . . .

CONTENTS

Introduction   page 7

Author's Note   10

Acknowledgements   10

SOUPS   11

FIRST COURSE   19

MAIN COURSE

Fish   37

Roasts   47

Casseroles   55

Pies   63

Miscellany of Meat Dishes   73

VEGETABLES AND SALADS   89

PUDDINGS   97

CAKES AND BISCUITS   125

LANZAROTE RECIPES   133

Index   139

First published in Great Britain by Hodder and Stoughton Ltd 1976
Copyright © Josceline Dimbleby 1976
Published by Sphere Books Ltd 1980

Printed in the United States of America

INTRODUCTION

Most cookery books are about a specific kind of food: food from a particular country, rich food for dinner parties, healthy country food for family life, cheap food, food you can make in a moment after a day at the office, food for people who live in one room or food for people who live in palaces, vegetarian food, seasonal food, regional food, very English food. I even have a book of food to be made entirely from flowers. There must be almost everything. So when I began to write this book I was asked what my theme was. All I can say is that it is a collection of my own ideas which I have made using flavours and consistencies which I like, and which I think taste delicious. The recipes range from spicy oriental dishes to nostalgic English nursery food, from family lunch food and teatime cakes to more unusual dishes for dinner parties.

As far as I can remember I have always loved food, though my mother assures me that as a young child I was pale and skinny and got no pleasure from eating at all. But I can vividly remember the smells and tastes of my travelling childhood and I am sure that early years spent in the Middle East and South America developed my passion for herbs, spices and strong, unusual flavours which I use in a lot of my cooking now. My husband has an adventurous taste in food and I am sure I would never have become such an enthusiastic cook if it had not been for his constant pleasure and interest in everything I try out. I do not make the food we eat any more bland for the children because I think it is important to develop and influence their taste buds from the very start. They certainly do not like everything I cook and when they go to school rather a battle begins because they want to conform with other fish-finger lovers, but luckily they are still curious to try out strange tastes. My oldest daughter loves snails and Camembert cheese but my son has a horrible passion for tomato ketchup with which he smothers everything. My youngest daughter who at the age of one ate really everything from the strongest curry to black-eyed octopus, now shows signs of becoming definitely fussy. All I want to avoid is that any of them should become one of those irritating children who make an insulting, sick face when anything other than chicken and peas is put in front of them. In any case I do find that it eases the daily drudge of preparing children's meals, and I hope improves their palates, if I take trouble with their food and give them varied and unusual things.

When I first started cooking I found it rather difficult to follow a recipe because I did not really know what I was doing or what I would produce. I found it easier to think of a delicious idea and then work out for myself how I could make it. This made me feel more confident and if I saw it going wrong it was up to me to try and do something about it so that it would still taste good. Once one or two of these ideas had worked I began to have many more, most of them dreamed up in my sleep. To my amazement I found that when I tried them out they really worked.

INTRODUCTION

When I learned more about cooking of course I was able to make better use of recipes. I could tell which would probably work, and my own ideas were now inspired not only by my dreams but by good ways of cooking which I was learning from books. The danger with recipes is that you give up your own responsibility for the dish; if you see that a piece of meat is burning in the oven after about an hour's cooking you are apt to let it go on burning just because the recipe says that it should cook for two hours! It is always important to remember that the way food cooks depends so much on its quality, its age and even the temperature of the air in your kitchen as you prepare it, so that a recipe can only be a guide. Your own judgment and instinct is always needed. Tasting and adjusting of seasoning is crucial too, especially the last taste before serving.

All my recipes can be varied and one aim of this book is to stimulate people to dare to try out ideas of their own and to experiment with different combinations of flavours instead of feeling that they always have to use a recipe. I have tried not to make any of the dishes too complicated to prepare, although good cooking does tend to take up time. It is worth taking trouble about the final appearance of the food, even choosing your serving dish carefully and seeing that its colour blends well with its contents. A moment or two spent adding a little pattern of fresh fruit on the top of a mousse, glazing a fruit tart with shiny redcurrant jelly, sprinkling some bright green fresh herbs on a rich stew just before serving or putting pastry patterns, even cut out messages, brushed with a gloss of egg yolk on top of a lovely pie, will make almost everyone gasp with admiration. It whets the appetite and gives great pleasure to people to be presented with a carefully prepared and beautiful dish.

I have made my recipes fairly detailed; experienced cooks may feel they do not need to be told so much, but friends so often say that recipes do not tell them enough. Long and elaborate recipes can also be off-putting. I hope I have struck a happy medium.

Most of the herbs and spices I use in these recipes can be bought at a delicatessen, a good grocer, or even a large supermarket. If you have an Indian grocer near you they should have jars full of exciting spices and it is useful to keep a collection of them. You can use dried herbs but fresh herbs are so much better: most of them are quite easy to grow at home, even in a window box,and nursery gardens usually sell a large variety of container grown herbs which you can plant in the spring or early summer and begin picking at once. It is so satisfying to use your own freshly picked feathery fennel and dill, to pull off a few pungent tarragon leaves or sprigs of aromatic thyme, while the intoxicating smell and flavour of fresh basil, reminiscent of Italian summer days, transforms a plain tomato salad. In the recipes where I have specified olive oil you can of course use other vegetable oils but for French dressing, mayonnaise and for the Mediterranean-type dishes in this book the taste of real olive oil makes all the difference and is worth the extra cost. But there are ways of saving money too. Ask your greengrocer for any old vegetables going cheap, which, even if they look limp, will have plenty of flavour for using in soups and stews. At the butcher, the fishmonger or the greengrocer look out for what is specially cheap that day and try making an experimental dish with it, instead of having a pre-fixed idea of what you are going to eat regardless of its cost.

Everyone organises their life differently. The only way I manage to fit in good cooking, entertaining, singing (a rival hobby to my cooking) and dealing with the insistent demands of three young children is by planning and thinking well ahead. It sounds boring to be so ordered but my life changed when instead of cooking all the food for a dinner party on one day I began preparing one or two dishes a day ahead. At last I had time to have a bath between the children's noisy bedtime and everyone arriving, and I was not so tired by the time we actually sat down to a meal that I could not speak. I also find that it makes the child-filled weekends much less exhausting if some of the cooking is done on Friday. But that is just my way. Disorder makes me lose confidence and give up. If I feel in control and if every step is clear in my head, or rather on my list, I am all right. I also get great pleasure from cooking if I can choose a time when there is no need to rush, preferably when there are no distracting children around, pulling at me, asking me questions and always wanting to try everything. Just a quiet, clean, sunny kitchen to work in and a colourful array of enticing ingredients. As I extol the pleasures of my kitchen life I think of several close friends who, although enthusiastic eaters, tell me that they really hate cooking – they feel it is time wasted and they rush through it as quickly as possible with no nice feeling of achievement or pride. It is difficult for me to know what to say to them but this book really began as a book of ideas written for friends, and if trying out my recipes makes anyone get even a little more enjoyment and interest out of cooking, I shall be very happy.

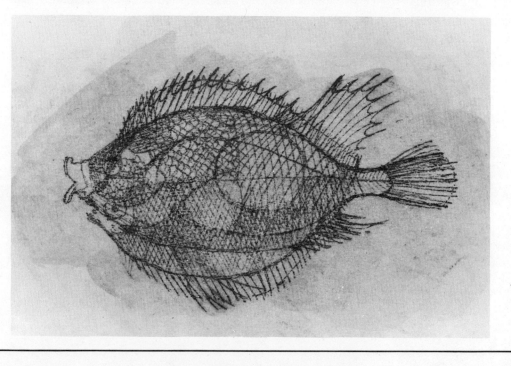

AUTHOR'S NOTE

The recipes in this book should all be enough for six people or for more where specified. The quantities are also fairly generous as the family and friends I have cooked them for are nearly all big eaters who will want second helpings.

When I have put a spoonful as a measure I mean a rounded spoonful unless I have said level or heaped.

Although I feel it is infinitely better to use fresh herbs if possible I realise that with some herbs, and in winter, you may have to use dried. Some are much better than others. Oregano, which I use a lot, still has a good flavour when it is dried, but it is not worth using dried basil. When I have given spoonful measurements for herbs you will probably need a really heaped spoonful of fresh herbs but only a level spoonful, or even less, if you are using dried.

If you have no home-made stock you can always use stock cubes. If you own a freezer I think it is most worthwhile making a large amount of stock from any bones, carcasses or vegetables you may have (the butcher will probably give you a bag of bones free) and freezing it in small amounts which you can use as you need them for soups and stews. If a recipe suggests long-grain rice I feel that the small Indian Basmati rice has much the best flavour. You can get it at delicatessens and oriental grocers. Being small, it takes less time to cook than ordinary rice, only 7–9 minutes in boiling water to reach the perfect, separate stage with a very slight bite to it. Risottos should traditionally be made with the round Italian rice but I have found that the cheaper pudding rice is a good substitute as long as you do not overcook it.

Rose water and orange flower water, which I find a delicious addition to fruit salads and milk or cream puddings, can be bought easily in chemists or Greek grocers. It is best to get the triple-strength kind and use only a little. Most large food halls sell both rose and violet essence. A featherlight fatless sponge flavoured with a drop or two of violet essence, filled with whipped violet flavoured cream and decorated with a sprinkling of sparkling castor sugar and crystallised violets is a romantic and delicious cake.

ACKNOWLEDGMENTS

I have been encouraged in the writing of this book by many friends but I would specially like to thank Carolyn Smith without whose enthusiastic help in transcribing the recipes and working out the index the preparation of A TASTE OF DREAMS would have been not a dream, but a nightmare.

SOUPS

Chilled Spinach Soup with Almonds   page 12
Halibut Soup with Pernod   12
Swede and Carrot Soup   13
Kipper and Tomato Soup   13
Cold (or Hot) Curried Fish Soup   14
Mushroom and Mustard Soup   15
Turnip and Spring Onion Soup   15
Nettle Soup   16
Tomato and Sorrel Soup with Lovage   17

Chilled Spinach Soup with Almonds

4 tins consommé (or jellied veal or
chicken stock if you have some)
¾ pint milk (425 ml)
about ½ lb spinach leaves (225 g)
handful of sorrel leaves (if available)
2 oz butter (50 g)
2 tablespoons plain flour

juice of 1 small lemon
¼ pint single cream (150 ml)
2 oz split blanched almonds (50 g)
fresh dill leaves to decorate (or parsley
if you cannot get any dill)
salt, black pepper

This is a thick summer soup which is not too rich or stodgy because what makes it thick is the cold jellied consommé or jellied stock you use. It tastes very good and has a really special flavour if you can use sorrel leaves as well, and get some fresh feathery dill leaves to sprinkle on the top with the almonds. It ought to be put into individual bowls and looks very summery and inviting.

If you have no blender chop the spinach up very finely, otherwise just roughly chop it. Melt the butter in a large heavy saucepan. Stir the chopped spinach into the butter. Stir in the flour. Heat the consommé or stock with the milk. Pour into the spinach saucepan and stir. Bring to the boil, stir and then simmer gently with a lid on for 15–20 minutes. Take off the stove, stir in the lemon juice, cool slightly and then whizz up in the blender. Add salt and black pepper to taste and transfer to individual dishes. Chill in the fridge for at least an hour. Before serving, pour some cream on to the soup in each dish but do not stir it in, and decorate with chopped dill leaves (or parsley) and the blanched split almonds.

Halibut Soup with Pernod   (serves 8)

2 oz butter (50 g)
2 tablespoons plain flour
1 lb filleted halibut (450 g)
juice of 1 lemon

a little Pernod
½ pint single cream (275 g)
finely chopped fennel leaves (fresh if
possible)
salt, pepper

I make this subtle, creamy soup with halibut because of its specially good flavour, but you can use any white fish. If you can get Greenland halibut it is much cheaper and will do just as well. Ask a sympathetic fishmonger for some good bones and scraps for the stock. You really need an electric blender for this soup.

Make stock by simmering fish bones, an unpeeled onion cut in half, 8 black peppercorns and salt in 4 pints of water (2¼ litres) for about an hour. Roughly chop fish. Melt butter in large saucepan. Take off heat. Stir in fish, then stir in flour. Add strained hot fish stock and stir. Put on lid and simmer for 20 minutes. Cool slightly. Whizz soup up in a blender and pour into another saucepan. Add cream, lemon juice, salt, pepper and Pernod to taste and gently re-heat. Stir in chopped fennel and serve.

Swede and Carrot Soup

1 small swede – about ½–¾ lb (225–
350 g)
1 lb carrots (450 g)
1 large clove garlic
3 pints chicken stock or stock and
water (1.7 litres)

juice of ½ lemon
½ pint single cream (275 ml)
salt, black pepper

*A nourishing and easy winter soup, but also very good cold in summer, made slightly
thicker with less stock.*

Peel and chop the vegetables and the garlic and cook in the stock for about half an hour
until soft. Cool and then whizz in a blender or put through a Mouli. Re-heat stirring in the
lemon juice and the single cream and adding the salt and black pepper. Be careful not to let
it boil.

Kipper and Tomato Soup

2 kipper fillets
1½ lb tomatoes – fresh or tinned (700 g)
2 tablespoons of plain flour
1 small clove garlic – crushed

1 pint hot milk (570 ml)
¼ pint single cream (150 ml)
salt, black pepper
2 oz butter (50 g)

*One day I had some kipper fillets which the children had not eaten and some squashy-
looking tomatoes, so I made them into a cream soup. I think the smoky kipper goes well
with the tomatoes – in fact you can't tell that it is kipper – it tastes like some much more
exotic fish soup.*

Cut up the kipper fillets into fairly small pieces. Dip the tomatoes in boiling water, skin them
and cut in half. Melt about 2 oz (50 g) butter in a large, heavy saucepan and take off heat.
Stir in the kipper pieces, the tomatoes, and the crushed garlic. Stir in the flour. Gradually
stir in the hot milk mixed with another half pint of water seasoned with salt and black
pepper. Put on the lid and simmer for about 20 minutes. Cool a little. Then cream the soup
in an electric blender or fine Mouli. Stir in the single cream and check salt and pepper
seasoning. Re-heat to serve or in the summer it is good chilled. I think that almost all
soups are better if you add a dash of lemon juice before serving, and I sometimes add a little
sherry to fish soups.

Cold (or hot) Curried Fish Soup

1 lb coley fillet — get the fishmonger to
skin it for you (450 g)
2 oz butter (50 g)
2 tablespoons plain flour
juice of ½ lemon
2—4 teaspoons curry powder
salt, pepper
¼ pint single cream (150 ml)
2 pints milk (a generous litre)
1 pint chicken stock (570 ml)
6 oz peeled prawns (175 g)

You really need a blender for this tasty, creamy soup. It is very cheap to make because you only need to use coley, almost the cheapest of fish, for the basis of it. I think it is worth getting a few peeled prawns to add at the end. If by any chance you have an enterprising greengrocer, fresh coriander leaves, chopped up and thrown on at the last minute are a very special addition.

Melt the butter in a large saucepan and remove from heat. Add the chopped coley fillets and stir so that the fish is coated with butter. Stir in the flour. Heat the milk and chicken stock and stir into the fish mixture. Bring to the boil, add curry powder, salt and pepper to taste and simmer, stirring often, for 15–20 minutes. Add the lemon juice. Cool slightly and then whizz it all up, until smooth and creamy, in the blender. Add the cream and the prawns, check for seasoning, and either re-heat carefully or serve chilled.

VARIATION. You can make a more Mediterranean version of this soup by adding a pinch of saffron and a clove of crushed garlic instead of the curry powder.

Mushroom and Mustard Soup

½–¾ lb mushrooms (225–350 g)
2–4 teaspoons mild French
mustard – to taste
1 pint single cream (150 ml)

1½ pints milk (845 ml)
juice of ½ large lemon or 1 small lemon
1 oz butter (25 g)
black pepper, salt

This soup is really easy and quick to make and I think it is a subtle combination of flavours – people always seem to sip up every drop so they must think so too. The mild whole seed mustard is much the best for this if you can get it.

Slice the mushrooms very thinly sideways keeping the stalks on so they make a mushroom shape. Melt the butter gently in a fairly large heavy based saucepan. Stir the mushrooms into the butter and cook gently for about a minute or two. Add the cream and the milk, salt, black pepper and the mustard. Heat but do not boil. When it is hot very gradually add the lemon juice, stirring all the time. This will thicken the soup. If you add the lemon juice too quickly it may curdle – you can uncurdle it by straining the liquid from the mushrooms and whizzing it in the blender for a moment or two. (You can uncurdle sauces in this way too.) Taste for seasoning and add extra salt and pepper or mustard if you feel it needs it. Serve the soup with crusty fresh bread, preferably warmed in the oven first.

Turnip and Spring Onion Soup

1 large or 2 medium-size
turnips – about 1–1½ lb (450–700 g)
¾ lb potatoes (350 g)
3 pints well-seasoned chicken stock
(1.7 litres)

salt, black pepper
bunch of spring onions
½ pint single cream (275 ml)

This is a very simple and delicious creamy soup, rather like Jerusalem artichoke soup but with a slightly more delicate flavour, and much easier to prepare. The combination of the rather watery consistency of the turnips and the denseness of potatoes makes a wonderfully smooth texture and the spring onions in it are crunchy and fresh tasting. It is equally good hot or cold.

Peel the turnips and potatoes and chop roughly. Boil them in the chicken stock for 20–30 minutes until very soft. Cool slightly and then whizz up in a blender until really smooth or put through a fine Mouli. Re-heat if you want it hot and add the single cream and more salt and pepper to taste. Chop the spring onions finely using most of the green part too, and stir them into the soup before serving. If you pour the soup into individual bowls either hot or cold, sprinkle with spring onions on top of each.

Nettle Soup

**bundle of nettles – approximately 1 lb
(450 g)**
1½ tablespoons plain flour
2 oz butter (50 g)
**about 3 pints of chicken stock (1.7
litres)**
juice of ½ large lemon
¼ pint sour cream (150 ml) (optional)
salt, black pepper

This is a most satisfying soup to make in these days when even potatoes are expensive because the main ingredient is completely free – young nettles are best but I have made the soup at the end of the summer with some rather tired nettles from my overgrown garden, and it still tasted good. Of course you must wear gloves to pick and prepare the nettles.

Pull the leaves off the nettle stems. If you do not have a blender chop up the leaves as small as possible. Melt the butter in a large saucepan. Take off heat. Put in the leaves and coat with butter. Stir in the flour. Pour in heated stock and stir well. Bring to the boil, stirring often. Simmer for 10–15 minutes. Add salt and black pepper to taste. If you have a blender put the soup in when it has cooled a bit, and blend. Stir in lemon juice and re-heat before serving. If liked add a drop of sour cream to each bowl of soup when serving out.

Tomato and Sorrel Soup with Lovage

1½ lb tomatoes — dipped in boiling
water and skinned (700 g)
15–20 sorrel leaves
1 large potato — about ½ lb (225 g)
2½ oz butter (60 g)
1 clove garlic — crushed
3 tablespoons tomato purée
about 10–15 lovage leaves
2 tablespoons flour
1 pint chicken stock (570 ml)
salt, black pepper
1½ pints of water (845 ml)

This is a good tomato and sorrel soup. The lovage, if you can get it, gives it a very special flavour. Though lovage is one of the oldest herbs it does not seem to grow in very many gardens — perhaps because it grows about six feet high and is less manageable than the more usual herbs. I find it easy to grow and it has a strong, unique flavour which is good in salads and for soups and stews. If you live in the country you will be able to find sorrel growing wild in a field or in your garden — the leaves look rather like spinach and you can identify them by their sour taste. But if you live in a city and do not grow sorrel in your back garden or even in a window box, then as second best you can substitute spinach leaves and the juice of a lemon.

Chop up the skinned tomatoes in small pieces. Chop up the sorrel leaves very finely. Cut the potato into small cubes. Melt the butter in a large, heavy saucepan and remove from heat. Stir the tomatoes, sorrel and potato into the butter. Stir in the flour. Heat together chicken stock with 1½ pints water (845 ml), the tomato purée, salt, pepper and the crushed garlic. Pour into the saucepan with the tomato mixture and bring to the boil stirring once or twice. Simmer gently for about ½ hour. Chop up the lovage leaves and add them about 5 minutes before you take the soup off the heat.

FIRST COURSES

Stripy Fish Fillets in Lemon Dressing   page 20
Smoked Mackerel Fillets with Smoked
   Cod's Roe Sauce   21
Deep Sea Tart   22
Spiced Sesame Fish Bites   23
Turmeric Pies   24
Curried Baskets Filled with Mushrooms in
   Mayonnaise   25
Mushrooms and Mint   26
Surprise Custard Marrows   26
Avocados with Cockles and Mussels   27
Devilled Pork Balls with Broad Beans   28
Cold Stuffed Peppers à l'Indienne   29
Curried Egg Loaf   30
Eggs Stuffed with Caviare and Cream Cheese 31
Eggs and Onion in Curried Cream Cheese
   Sauce   31
Eggs with Almond and Spring Onion Stuffing 32
Almond and Onion Chilli Puff   33
Special Terrine of Rabbit with Prunes   34
Kipper Pâté   35

Stripy Fish Fillets in Lemon Dressing

1 lb cod fillets (with any black skin taken
off) (450 g)
¾ lb carrots (350 g)
1 tin of anchovies (optional)
juice of 1 small lemon
3–4 tablespoons olive oil
2 teaspoons French mustard
(preferably the whole seed type)
small bunch fresh chives – or parsley
1 teaspoon honey
salt, black pepper

I think cold fish first courses are often a good idea because they can taste really delicious but in no way fill you up. This is a dish which you can make very pretty with the fish and carrots arranged in stripes or in circles on a round dish – and it can be made well in advance.

Smear a little olive oil all over the cod, put it in a covered oiled ovenproof dish and bake in the oven at Gas 6 (400°F/200°C) for 20 minutes. Take out and let it go cold. Meanwhile, wash and scrape the carrots well and boil them whole in salted water until done. Drain them and let them go cold. When the fish and carrots are cold cut them both into fairly thin strips with a sharp knife and arrange them in stripes in any pattern you like on a shallow serving dish. Put an anchovy fillet on top of each piece of cod. In an empty jam jar with a lid put the honey, the mustard, a good pinch of salt, plenty of black pepper, the lemon juice and the olive oil. You should have about one third lemon juice to two thirds olive oil. Shake up vigorously and pour the dressing all over the fish and carrots. Chop the chives (or parsley) finely and sprinkle on top. Serve with buttered brown bread.

Smoked Mackerel Fillets with Smoked Cod's Roe Sauce

1 large or 2 smaller mackerel
8 oz cream cheese (225 g)
about 4 oz smoked cod's roe (110 g)
single cream or top of the milk
black pepper, salt
parsley or fennel leaves to decorate
juice of ½ lemon

Smoked mackerel can be bought or ordered from most good fishmongers – it is always moist and full of flavour. It is good eaten just filleted with lemon juice squeezed over it. But for a change this is a delicious way to use it.

Cut the mackerel open and take out the flesh leaving the skin and bones. Arrange the pieces of fish in a shallow dish. Into a bowl put the cream cheese, smoked cod's roe (if you buy it in a piece take the skin off first) and the lemon juice and mash up very thoroughly with a fork; if you have a liquidiser it is much easier to do it in that and makes a smoother sauce. Add a lot of black pepper and a small pinch of salt and mix it in. Now if it is still very thick gradually add cream or top of the milk until it is creamier and you are able to pour it all over the smoked fish. Decorate with parsley or feathery fennel (fennel is really worth growing either in your garden or even a window box as it is very pretty for decoration and delicious chopped up in salads, sprinkled over cooked vegetables or cooked with fish).

Deep Sea Tart

(serves 6–8)

FOR THE PASTRY CRUST
8 oz plain flour (225 g)
4 oz soft margarine or butter (110 g)
2 oz lard (50 g)
1 large egg – beaten

FOR THE FILLING
¾ lb squid (350 g)
1 large or 2 small avocado pears
3 oz peeled prawns (75 g)
½ pint double cream (275 ml)
1 teaspoon powdered mace, or
powdered nutmeg
juice of ½ small lemon
1 clove of garlic – crushed
salt, black pepper
butter and oil to fry in

This is a cold savoury tart with a delicious creamy filling of subtly flavoured squid with avocados and prawns. If you have never tasted squid, it is mild and delicious and sold fresh now in several fishmongers. This is a pretty-looking dish and good for parties too.

To make the pastry cut the fat into the flour and rub in lightly with your fingertips until it resembles breadcrumbs. Mix in the beaten egg with a knife. Gather into a ball and refrigerate for an hour or more. Then roll out and line a buttered 9–10 in shallow flan dish (23–25.5 cm), preferably the aluminium kind with the lifting out base. Heat oven to fairly hot, Gas 6 (400°F/200°C). Put a piece of foil across the pastry, weight it down with dried beans or rice and bake blind for about 20 minutes until cooked. Cut any extra pastry into little rounds or shapes and cook at the same time as the tart (though they may cook a bit quicker), and use them to decorate with later. Take out and cool.

Chop the squid into very small pieces. (You may have to extract a strange transparent bone but all else is edible, though you may like to leave out the goggling black eyes!) Fry gently in a little olive oil and butter for about 10 minutes. Transfer to a mixing bowl. Add 2 oz (50 g) of the prawns (reserve the rest) and the avocado pear peeled and cut into chunks. Stir the powdered mace, the crushed garlic, the lemon juice, salt and black pepper into the cream and stir into the fish mixture. Heat oven to moderate Gas 5 (375°F/190°C). Pour the creamy mixture into the pastry case and put back in the oven for 8 minutes. Decorate with the remainder of the prawns and the pastry shapes if you have them. Serve cool.

Spiced Sesame Fish Bites

¾ lb filleted white-skinned plaice
(350 g)
1 teaspoon powdered coriander
2–3 teaspoons powdered ginger
1 teaspoon powdered cardamom
1 teaspoon powdered cumin
1 clove garlic – crushed
salt to taste
1 small egg – lightly beaten
about 2 oz sesame seeds (50 g)
a handful of roughly chopped
parsley – or if you have an Indian grocer
who has fresh coriander leaves they are
really good for this recipe

FOR THE SAUCE
½ pint plain yoghurt (275 ml)
3–4 teaspoons Patak's Tikka paste – or
a combination of spices used in the fish
balls plus 1–2 teaspoons lemon juice
salt, black pepper

This is an appetising first course of hot curried fish balls rolled in sesame seeds and dressed with oil and lemon, served with cold spiced yoghurt sauce. They can be made in advance and re-heated or kept hot until you are ready to eat them. If you have not got all the spices just use the ones you have, even if you have only got curry powder. Patak's Tikka paste which is used in the sauce is worth looking for in an Indian grocer's. It is milder and much better tasting than usual curry pastes and is very useful for brushing over meat and chicken which you are going to grill or barbecue, as well as adding to curries and sauces. If you can't get it for this sauce you can use a combination of the spices used in the fish balls.

Put the fish through a mincer or if you have not got one cut it up as small as possible. Mix the fish and the salt, crushed garlic and spices into a mixing bowl together. Stir in the lightly beaten egg thoroughly. Spread the sesame seeds out on to a large board. Gather the fish mixture up into small balls and roll lightly on the seame seeds so that they are thinly coated. Brush the bottom of a roasting pan with oil and put in the balls. Spoon a little oil on top of each and bake in the centre of the oven at Gas 5 (375°F/190°C) for 20–25 minutes. Remove the balls from the roasting pan, leaving behind any juice that has come out of them during cooking. Arrange them on a shallow serving dish and keep warm. Mix up a dressing of one third lemon juice, two thirds olive oil, salt and pepper. Just before serving, pour the dressing over the fish balls and sprinkle them with parsley, or coriander leaves. Serve with a bowl of yoghurt sauce which you have mixed up beforehand.

Turmeric Pies

FOR THE PASTRY
12 oz plain flour (350 g)
6 oz butter or block margarine (175 g)
3 oz lard (75 g)
2 teaspoons turmeric
pinch of salt
a little very cold water

FOR THE FILLING
8 oz full fat cream cheese (225 g)
$\frac{1}{2}$ teaspoon chilli powder
1–2 cloves of garlic – crushed
salt, black pepper

FOR THE SOUR-CREAM SAUCE
$\frac{1}{4}$ pint soured cream (150 ml)
$\frac{1}{4}$ pint plain yoghurt (150 ml)

These little yellow pies with a soft cream cheese and chilli filling make a pretty and unusual first course. Served warm with a cold fresh tasting soured cream sauce they melt in the mouth and are delicious.

Sift the flour, salt and turmeric into a mixing bowl. Cut in the fat and crumble the mixture with your fingertips until it resembles breadcrumbs. With a round-bladed knife mix in a very little cold water until the mixture just sticks together. Gather into a ball and put in the fridge for at least an hour.

Put the filling ingredients into a bowl and mix thoroughly together with a fork. To make the pies, roll out the pastry fairly thickly, about $\frac{1}{4}$ in ($\frac{1}{2}$ cm). Use a 3 in (7.5 cm) round fluted cutter and cut out 12 rounds, then a $2\frac{1}{4}$ in ($5\frac{1}{2}$ cm) round cutter and cut out another 12 rounds. Re-roll the pastry as necessary. Line some greased patty tins with the large rounds. Spoon some cheese filling into each round. Moisten the underside of the smaller rounds and put on top, pressing down lightly at the edges. Cut a small slit in each. Brush with milk and bake in the centre of the oven for about 20 minutes at Gas 7 (425°F/220°C). Leave them to cool in the tins for 5 minutes or so and then gently – as the pastry is deliciously crumbly – ease them out with a round-bladed knife. Serve warm, garnished with some watercress and parsley. Combine the soured cream and yoghurt in a bowl, sprinkle with a tiny pinch of chilli powder and pass the sauce round to spoon over the pies.

Curried Baskets Filled with Mushrooms in Mayonnaise

FOR THE PASTRY
Make one quantity of the curried version of the cheese straw recipe (page 131)

FOR THE FILLING
½–¾ lb mushrooms (225–350 g)
about ¼ pint mayonnaise (150 ml). If you are really in a hurry a good commercial kind like Hellman's Real Mayonnaise is quite all right for this.
handful of fresh chopped herbs — dill is very good with this, basil, mint or parsley.

This is an original cold first course which looks quite elaborate. The baskets are made with the feather-light pastry of the cheese straws recipe (page 131) and although they seem slightly fiddly to do the first time it is really worth it for their appearance and taste. You need 12 fairy cake or patty tins and a round, fluted pastry cutter approximately 3 in (7.5 cm) diameter.

Pastry made to the curried version of the cheese straws recipe (page 131). Same quantity.

Roll out the pastry and cut out 12 rounds with the fluted cutter. Press them gently down into the ungreased fairy cake tins. Pre-heat oven to Gas 7 (425°F/220°C). Tear off small pieces of greaseproof paper or foil and put a piece on each uncooked pastry tart. Then weigh each down with some dried beans or rice and bake "blind" in the top half of the oven for approximately 10 minutes. Take out paper and beans and put back in the oven for a further 3 minutes. Let cool.

TO MAKE THE FILLING. Chop up the mushrooms quite small, stalks and all, and put into a mixing bowl. Mix the chopped fresh herbs with the mushrooms (reserving just a few herbs for final decoration) and add enough mayonnaise to envelop and bind together all the mushrooms. Fill the curried baskets (2 for each person) with the mixture and sprinkle a very few fresh herbs on the top of each one. If possible, delay making up the filling until shortly before the meal and then leave the filled baskets in a cool place, but not in the fridge, until you are ready to eat.

Mushrooms and Mint

¾ lb small mushrooms (350 g)
2 small onions
large handful of fresh mint leaves
3 cloves of garlic — crushed or chopped finely

5 tablespoons olive oil
juice of one lemon
wine vinegar
salt, black pepper

This is a very simple summer first course, quick to make and good to taste!

Into a saucepan pour the olive oil, the juice of a small lemon and about a tablespoonful of wine vinegar. Then put in a lot of freshly ground black pepper, a spoonful of salt, 3 cloves of garlic put through a garlic press (or chopped very finely if you haven't got one), the mint leaves roughly chopped up, the mushrooms sliced and the onions peeled and cut into very thin rings. Mix all this up with a spoon and put on a very low heat with the lid on for not more than 10 minutes. Pour into a serving dish and cool in the fridge. Serve with brown bread so that greedy people can mop up any remaining juice with it.

Surprise Custard Marrows

one small custard marrow per person
one egg yolk per person
peeled tomatoes — about one per person

chopped fresh basil if possible — or thyme, oregano or marjoram
a little oil and vinegar dressing
salt, black pepper

I think this is a quite original, cold first course. Unfortunately, custard marrows are only in season between August and October and then only sold by good greengrocers and markets. They look like little pies with scalloped edges and are far superior in taste and texture to ordinary marrows. If you do find them you may like to know an interesting recipe for them. They vary a lot in size and although only the smallest kind are any good for this way of stuffing them with egg yolks; you could make another stuffing like ratatouille for the larger kind, which would each feed 2 – 3 people. Plan to have meringues or an Angel cake for pudding.

Cut the stalks off the marrows and scoop out the insides – pips etc, with a teaspoon. Put them in a saucepan of boiling, salted water. Cover pan and simmer for 20 minutes. Take out carefully and drain. Heat oven to Gas 6 (400°F/200°C). Salt and pepper the insides of the marrows. Separate the egg yolks and put one inside each marrow. Slightly mush up the tomatoes and mix with herbs, salt and pepper. Pile mixture on top of the egg yolks. Sprinkle with grated Parmesan. Put marrows on baking tray in the centre of the oven for 20 minutes. Take out and cool in fridge. When cold and just before serving, spoon a little oil and vinegar dressing over them. They are really delicious and the surprise is when the egg yolk bursts out as people take their second mouthful.

Avocados with Cockles and Mussels

3 avocados
4 oz cockles (110 g)
6 oz mussels (175 g)
about ½ pint home-made mayonnaise
with garlic (275 g)
¼ pint extra thick double cream or
whipped cream (150 ml)
bunch parsley — finely chopped
salt, black pepper

This is a quickly made stuffing for avocados which is a nice change from the usual prawns or vinaigrette.

Soak the cockles and mussels in cold water for at least half an hour to get rid of excess vinegar. Rinse and drain. Stir the cream, salt and black pepper to taste into the mayonnaise and add the cockles, mussels and the finely chopped parsley. Cut the avocados in half and pile the mixture into each. Decorate with a sprig of parsley.

Devilled Pork Balls with Broad Beans

1 lb minced pork (450 g)
2 level teaspoons powdered coriander
seeds
2 level teaspoons powdered cumin
seeds
1 level teaspoon chilli powder
2 tablespoons tomato purée
a good handful of chopped fresh mint
leaves
1 egg – lightly whisked
salt, pepper
lemon juice
olive oil
5–6 oz broad beans – frozen will do
(150–175 g)

I think this is best as a cold first course though you can serve it hot if you like. The spicy taste of the little meat balls goes well with the smoothness of the broad beans. The golden brown and pale green arranged on the dish under the gloss of an oil and lemon dressing is pretty and appetising.

In a mixing bowl mix up thoroughly with a wooden spoon the minced pork, the spices, the tomato purée, the mint leaves, the lightly whisked egg and a little salt and pepper. Smear a little oil on the bottom of a roasting pan. Form the meat mixture into very small balls and put in the roasting pan. Cook in the centre of the oven at Gas 4 (350°F/180°C) for 30 minutes. Transfer the meat balls, leaving behind any juices and fat that have exuded from them, on to a fairly large, shallow serving dish. Boil the broad beans and arrange them on the dish among the meat balls. Cool. Before serving mix up a dressing of one third lemon juice, two thirds olive oil, and a little salt and pepper. Spoon it over the dish. A sprinkling of chopped mint leaves or parsley or if you can get them a few fresh bean sprouts on top look pretty. Also if you can get it the flat unleavened Arab bread is just right with this.

Cold Stuffed Red Peppers à l'Indienne

6–12 small red peppers (12 if very
small, 6 if a bit larger)
1 cup Basmati rice
2 cups water
1 teaspoon turmeric
¾ lb minced lamb (350 g)
3–4 teaspoons curry power
2 teaspoons powdered cumin
2 teaspoons powdered cardamom
2 cloves garlic – crushed
1 tablespoon tomato purée
salt, black pepper
olive oil
wine vinegar

You will probably have realised how much I like the spices most used in Indian cookery. Stuffed peppers can be quite a boring dish but if you can get very small red peppers this cold spicy version tastes delicious and looks beautiful arranged on crisp green lettuce or spinach leaves as a first course, or as one of the cold dishes at a large party. I think Basmati rice has much the best flavour and you can get it at Indian shops and delicatessens. As it is smaller it needs less cooking than normal long grain rice.

First soak the rice in cold water for at least half an hour and drain. Take just the tops off the peppers and any pips etc, from inside. Put them in boiling salted water for 5 minutes. Drain and put on one side. Add ½ teaspoon salt and the turmeric to the 2 cups of water and bring to the boil. Stir in the soaked rice, cover and simmer gently for 6–10 minutes – test constantly and do not go away as the rice should be only just tender, not really soft. Empty rice into a sieve and rinse under cold water. Put on one side. Season the mince with the spices and curry powder, salt and black pepper. Heat a little olive oil in a frying pan, add the mince mixture, the tomato purée and garlic and fry fairly quickly for about 3–5 minutes, digging at the meat with a wooden spoon to keep it separate. Mix the meat with the rice. Press the meat and rice mixture compactly into the peppers with a teaspoon. Put the stuffed peppers into a fireproof dish with a very little olive oil, cover with foil and bake in the centre of a pre-heated oven Gas 5 (375°F/190°C) for 30–40 minutes according to the size of the peppers. When cold arrange, tops upwards, on some crisp green lettuce leaves on a pretty dish and spoon an oil and vinegar dressing over them just before serving.

Curried Egg Loaf (and variations)

1 thin sliced brown loaf
¾ lb full fat cream cheese (350 g). If you
can't find any at your delicatessen or at
a large supermarket Kraft Philadelphia
will do.
2 oz melted butter (50 g)
6 medium-boiled eggs
2 teaspoons curry powder (or to taste)
a little salt
lemon juice

This is a very good first course for dinner parties or as one of the dishes at a larger party. It is easy to make but looks unusual, and all the variations taste really good. I give the quantities for a medium-sized bread loaf tin which will feed six to eight people. You really need a liquidiser for this dish and it is better to make it well before you need it as it must get very cold.

In a liquidiser (you will probably have to do it in two or three lots and put it in a bowl) blend the cream cheese, the boiled eggs, the curry powder, a pinch of salt, the melted butter and the lemon juice until smooth. Check for taste and add more curry powder and salt if you want to. Now cut the crusts off the sliced brown bread. Butter a 2 lb (1 kg) bread tin and put a layer of bread on the bottom, cutting it to fit the tin exactly. Now spread a thick layer of the cream cheese mixture and so on to the very top of the tin ending with a layer of bread. Now put the tin in the fridge for several hours or overnight. Before serving turn loaf out on to a plate and decorate with sprigs of parsley or anything you like. If it will not turn out easily dip it briefly into a sink of very hot water and then it should slip out. It is a dish which freezes well but if you keep it for long in the freezer it should be in a suitably shaped non-metal container. You can turn it out frozen by doing the hot water dip and it will thaw out to serve in about two hours. When you slice it it looks like a smooth pâté with strips of bread incorporated in it and tastes very good.

VARIATIONS
Sardine loaf. Instead of the eggs and curry powder, mix the cream cheese etc, with a tin of sardines and some black pepper and proceed as before.
Kipper Loaf. Mix one or two cooked kipper fillets with the cream cheese, salt, black pepper, lemon juice and butter and proceed as before.
Smoked Salmon Loaf. Mix about ¼ lb chopped smoked salmon (110 g) with the cream cheese, salt, black pepper, lemon juice and butter and proceed as before. Garnish the top with a few prawns.

Eggs Stuffed with Caviare and Cream Cheese

6 large eggs
6 oz cream cheese (175 g)
¼ pint of soured cream (150 ml)
1 small pot of Danish caviare (lump fish
roe)
black pepper, pinch of salt

Of course this is not made with real caviare, just the famous lump fish roe! But it is very quick to make and looks and tastes good.

Semi hard boil the eggs (about 7 minutes). Cut in half and scoop out yolks with a teaspoon and put into a mixing bowl. Arrange whites in a shallow serving dish. Put cream cheese, soured cream and a pinch of salt into the mixing bowl and mash all up with a fork until it is like a very thick cream. Stir in the caviare and spoon the mixture into each half of an egg. Decorate with sprigs of parsley, chill and serve.

Eggs and Onion in Curried Cream Cheese Sauce

8 large eggs
¼ pint single cream (150 ml)
2 small onions
6 oz cream cheese (175 g)
1-2 teaspoon curry powder
salt, black pepper

You can make this easy dish with or without the raw onion. If you are doing it in large quantities for parties I would leave out the onion as it can go watery if it is made too far in advance, but if you make the dish on the day of eating the onion makes a good difference.

Hard boil the eggs. Slice them thinly and arrange in a shallow dish. Slice up the onions thinly and arrange among the eggs. Into a liquidiser put the cream cheese, the single cream, about one or two teaspoons of curry powder, a little black pepper and a pinch of salt. Whizz up until it is like a thick sauce — if it is too thick add bit more single cream if you have it, or top of the milk. Pour on to the eggs and onions. You need not make this sauce in a liquidiser, you can beat it up by hand but of course it takes much longer. Finally decorate with a sprinkling of paprika, or fennel leaves, or parsley. Chill in the fridge before serving.

Eggs with Almond and Spring Onion Stuffing

6 large eggs
2–3 oz ground almonds (50–75 g)
dessertspoon fresh marjoram – or
dried oregano
2 cloves of garlic – crushed
1 teaspoon mild French mustard
2–4 tablespoons olive oil
juice of 1 small lemon
small bunch of spring onions – chopped finely
cress or parsley as a garnish
salt, black pepper
a little oil and vinegar

These eggs are so easy to do and yet taste unusual and delicious with their mixture of consistencies. Since they look decorative, and can be prepared in advance and kept in a cool larder or the fridge for a day or two, they are useful both for dinner parties and as cold party food for a lot of people.

Hard boil the eggs and cool. Take the shells off the eggs and slice them in half lengthways. Scoop out the yolks into a bowl. Mash the yolks with a fork, add some olive oil and a little lemon juice. Mash in the ground almonds with the crushed garlic and the mustard. Gradually add more oil and lemon juice until it is a smooth, thick mixture. Mix in the marjoram and the finely chopped spring onions. Season to taste with salt and black pepper. Lay the eggs on a pretty dish on a bed of cress or parsley and stuff each one with a spoonful of the almond mixture. If by any chance you have any feathery fennel leaves in your garden a little of this on top of each egg looks lovely. Just before serving spoon a very little oil and vinegar dressing over the eggs to make them shiny and enticing.

Almond and Onion Chilli Puff

1 lb puff pastry (450 g)
3–4 large onions
2–3 tablespoons oil
1 heaped teaspoon ground cumin
½ teaspoon turmeric powder
¼–½ level teaspoon chilli powder – to taste
just under 1 tablespoon lemon juice
2 oz sultanas (50 g)
2–3 oz whole blanched almonds (50–75 g)
handful fresh mint or parsley leaves – chopped roughly
1 small egg yolk
salt

An unusual first course with an Indian flavour. It is easy to make but looks beautiful as the delicious spiced filling of onions and nuts tumbles out of the golden glazed puff pastry case. You can make it in advance and re-heat it or serve it almost cold which tastes very good too. A bowl of natural yoghurt to use as a sauce goes well.

Make the filling first. Peel and chop the onions. Fry them gently in the oil until they are soft and transparent. Stir in the spices, a sprinkling of salt, sultanas and the lemon juice. Transfer mixture to a bowl to cool. Heat another small spoonful of oil in the frying pan and toss the almonds very briefly in it until they go golden brown. Mix them into the onion mixture and lastly stir in the chopped mint or parsley leaves. When the mixture is cold cut the pastry in half and roll out two rounds about 8–9 in (20–23 cm) diameter – you can use a plate as a guide – and about ⅛ in (3 mm) thick. Lay one round on a damp baking tray or large ovenproof dish. Pile the onion filling on this pastry round leaving 1 in (2.5 cm) uncovered round the edges. Moisten this edge and place the other round of pastry on top and press down the edges to seal. Decorate with pastry trimmings and brush all over with egg yolk. Bake the pie in the centre of a pre-heated oven at Gas 8 (450°F/230°C) for 15 minutes and then Gas 6 (400°F/200°C) for a further 15 minutes. Serve hot or almost cold with a bowl of plain yoghurt as a sauce if liked.

Special Terrine of Rabbit with Prunes

(serves 10–14)

6 oz Californian prunes – soaked
overnight in about 2 glasses of red wine
(175 g)
2 lb leg of rabbit or 1½ lb boneless rabbit
(900 or 700 g) – you can buy boned
rabbit in frozen blocks at Sainsbury's; it
is called boneless Chinese rabbit and is
most useful for casseroles etc.
1 lb belly of pork (450 g)
½ lb stewing veal (225 g)
¾ lb smoked streaky bacon – thinly
sliced with rind removed (350 g)
3–4 whole juniper berries
1 tablespoon sage – finely chopped
1 tablespoon oregano or marjoram

powdered mace – Fox's herbs and
spices do this and probably others, it is
useful to have for adding to cakes and
puddings as well as for savoury dishes
salt, pepper

FOR THE MARINADE
about ½ wineglass brandy
juice of 1 orange
10–15 juniper berries – crushed
about 8 peppercorns
about 4 bayleaves
10–15 whole allspice – crushed
1 teaspoon salt

There is a small, unpretentious restaurant in the unfashionable Twelfth Arondissement of Paris called Chez Marcel where they specialise in terrines, pâté and saucissons of every kind. It is a plain "serious eaters" restaurant – my favourite kind of place – where all the clientele talk enthusiastically about food as they eat. Immediately you are settled at your table about ten different kinds of terrine and pâté are put in front of you, all of which you are supposed to try. This terrine is inspired by the one I enjoyed most at Chez Marcel the evening we went there. The only criticism I have of French terrines is that sometimes they do not seem to be flavoured strongly enough and are too bland for their richness. This rabbit, pork and veal terrine is very fully flavoured and I think, delicious. You must start to prepare it at least two days in advance but it is very satisfying to make and once it is made will keep for about two weeks in the fridge. You can serve it as a first course with hot toast, or as a main course with new or jacket potatoes and a mixed salad, and of course it is perfect for a party as it looks so beautiful, and feeds many.

Cut the flesh off the rabbit bones and chop into fairly small pieces. Put in a shallow pan with all the marinade ingredients and turn the rabbit well in the liquid. Cover and leave in a cool place for about 8 hours or overnight, stir the rabbit in the liquid once or twice during the marinating. Cut the rind off the belly of pork and put both the pork and the veal through the coarse blade of a mincer or cut up finely if you have no mincer. Season the meat with salt and pepper. Grease a 2-pint (1-litre) earthenware dish. Remove the bayleaves from the marinade and arrange them on the bottom of the dish in a pattern with 3 or 4 whole juniper berries. Lay the bacon neatly in strips on the bottom and sides of the dish, reserving enough to put on top of the terrine. Remove the stones from the soaked prunes with your fingers. Now proceed in layers; first a layer of rabbit, then a sprinkling of herbs and a little mace, then a few prunes, then a layer of pork and veal, then the herbs and mace again, then prunes, then rabbit and so on until all is used up. Pour over any left over marinating juices. Lay 2 bay leaves on the top and then the remaining strips of bacon. Cover with greased foil and then a lid and put the dish in a pan of water in the oven at Gas 3 (325°F/160°C) for 1½–2 hours or until a skewer stuck in the centre comes out clean. Cool for half an hour. It will smell delicious. Put a board on top of the foil (some juice will spill over when you do this, try to reserve it as it will turn into jelly to glaze the top when you finally turn the terrine out) and then some weights or books. Leave it weighted down for several hours or overnight if you can. Chill it in the fridge and then turn it out on to a serving dish. The easiest way to do this I have found is to dip the dish in very hot water in the sink – the water should just come up to the top of the dish – for about 1 minute or until the terrine plops out when you turn it upside down and give it a good shake. Now it should look a triumph and you will feel very pleased and clever. To perfect it slightly melt the reserved jelly juice if you have it and brush the top of the terrine with it, the sides should still have jelly sticking to them unless you left the dish in the hot water for too long. Return to the fridge until you serve it.

Kipper Pâté

8 oz full cream cheese (225 g). This should be the real full cream cheese which you can usually buy loose at a delicatessen or a large supermarket, but Kraft Philadelphia will do.
2–3 kipper fillets
butter
olive oil
1 clove of garlic – crushed
juice of ½ to 1 lemon
black pepper

Kipper pâté is economical, easy and always popular. There are lots of recipes for it, but I think the addition of cream cheese in this one makes it especially good.

Cook the kipper fillets by baking with a knob of butter for 15–20 minutes in a medium oven, Gas 4 (350°F/180°C). Then mash up with a fork as much as possible. Put cream cheese, about 1 oz melted butter, a tablespoon of olive oil, 1 crushed large clove of garlic, the juice of ½ a large lemon, quite a lot of coarsely ground black pepper and the mashed kipper into a mixing bowl and mix all together very well indeed. Put into a small serving bowl (it looks nice in earthenware) and put in the fridge for an hour or so. Serve it as a first course with brown toast or like an American "dip" at parties. This quantity will serve six or even eight but even if you give it to only four it usually gets eaten up because it really is good!

MAIN COURSE: FISH

Mackerel en Papillote with Tarragon and Caper   page
   Sauce   38
Scallops and Prawns in Garlic Cheese Sauce with
   Sesame Top   39
Noodles with Seafood and Garlic Sauce   40
Spinach Wrapped Fish Fillets in Pastry Parcels   41
Fillets of Cod in Rich Beetroot Sauce   42
Mediterranean Fish Casserole   43
Mussels Gratinée   44
Souffléed Fish Pie   45
Stuffed Fillets of Plaice   45
Smoked Mackerel Quiche   46

Mackerel en Papillote with Tarragon and Caper Sauce

1 fairly small mackerel per person
– gutted but with heads left on
1–2 bay leaves per fish
butter

FOR THE SAUCE
about 1 tablespoon finely chopped
tarragon
2–3 teaspoons capers – roughly
chopped
1 teaspoon French mustard
1 oz butter (25 g)
1 oz cornflour (25 g)
¾ pint milk (425 ml)
1 egg yolk – beaten lightly
a little cream or top of the milk
salt, black pepper

Baking individual fish wrapped in their own little paper parcels keeps in all the flavour and juices and looks exciting. Mackerel has remained comparatively cheap and being an oily fish is very nutritious, moist textured and full of flavour. If you can get fresh tarragon for the sauce it makes a lot of difference but dried will do.

Cut a piece of greaseproof paper to wrap each fish up in and butter the paper. Put the bay leaves inside the fish where they have been gutted. Wrap each fish up in paper and twist the ends to seal. Bake on a baking sheet or tray in the centre of the oven at Gas 5 (375°F/190°C) for 20–25 minutes.

Melt the butter in a saucepan. Take off the heat and blend in the cornflour. Stir in the milk. Bring to the boil and simmer gently for 3 minutes, stirring. Add salt, pepper, tarragon, capers and mustard and simmer another minute. Take off the heat, stir in a little cream and lightly beaten egg yolk and pour into a sauce jug. Serve with the mackerel. It is best to put the paper parcels on each person's plate; they can unwrap them and push the fish gently off the paper – you will need a bowl or a bin nearby for the discarded paper. Broccoli would go very well with this, and some new or plain boiled potatoes.

Scallops and Prawns in Garlic Cheese Sauce with Sesame Top

6 scallops or ¾ lb frozen scallops (350 g)
6 oz peeled prawns (175 g)
½–¾ lb mushrooms (225–350 g)
1 large pimento (red if possible)
1½ pints milk (845 ml)
1½ oz cornflour (40 g)
1½ oz butter (40 g)
2 large cloves garlic – crushed
6 oz grated cheese (175 g)
2 egg yolks
about 2 tablespoons of sesame seeds
pinch of saffron or a teaspoon of powered turmeric
fennel leaves – fresh if possible but otherwise dried
salt, black pepper
a little olive oil and butter to fry in

This is a very delicious and popular dish. It is impressive for dinner parties and is not difficult, although it has several ingredients which have to be cooked separately. But it can be prepared well in advance and heated up if necessary. I would do those flat egg noodles, well buttered, with it, and a crisp cos lettuce, parsley and tomato salad with perhaps some crusty bread to mop up the sauce. If there are no scallops about it tastes very good with the frozen ones you get in frozen food centres. If you have any saffron it is specially good for the sauce, but saffron is expensive so you can just use turmeric if you like or neither.

Add the crushed garlic, salt and pepper to 1 pint of milk (570 ml) and simmer the scallops in it for 15–20 minutes. Take out the scallops reserving the milk they were cooked in and arrange with the prawns in a large ovenproof gratinée dish. Chop up the pimento into small strips and fry gently in a little olive oil and butter until soft. Add to the scallops and prawns. Cut the mushrooms in half and sauté them in the same pan until just cooked, do not leave them until they shrink too much. Add these to the other ingredients in the gratinée dish and sprinkle with chopped fennel leaves. Melt 1½ oz butter (40 g) in a fairly heavy saucepan. Remove from the heat and stir in the cornflour and then the milk the scallops were cooked in and another ½ pint (275 ml). Bring to the boil, stirring. Stir in the cheese and saffron and simmer gently for about 3 minutes. Remove from the heat. Break the egg yolks with a fork, stir a little sauce into them quickly and then stir this mixture back into the main bulk of the sauce. Add salt and black pepper to taste. Pour the sauce over the mixture in the gratinée dish. Sprinkle the sesame seeds thickly all over the top, dot with butter and put under a hot grill until golden brown all over. Put the dish in a very low oven Gas ½ (175°F/80°C) for about half an hour before serving.

Noodles with Seafood and Garlic Sauce

10–12 oz flat egg noodles (275–350 g)
½–¾ lb peeled prawns (225–350 g)
1 lb squid or other seafood (450 g)
6 oz small mushrooms – sliced very
finely downwards (175 g)
olive oil
3 oz butter (75 g)

FOR THE SAUCE
½ pint single cream (275 ml)
large clove garlic – crushed
2 eggs – beaten
salt, black pepper

This creamy, flavourful bowl of noodles is always very popular. Don't recoil from the shiny goggle-eyed appearance of squid on your fishmonger's slab. It has a delicate and delicious taste.

Chop the squid (you may have to remove a strange plastic-like transparent bone, but the fishmonger should have removed the ink bag and innards) into very small pieces with a sharp knife, tentacles and all. Melt a mixture of olive oil and 3 oz butter (75 g) in a large pan and gently fry the squid for about 10 minutes. Stir in the prawns, salt and pepper. Stir in the sliced mushrooms. Put the mixture in a covered dish in a low oven to keep warm. Boil the noodles in plenty of salted water in an open saucepan until soft. Drain, put in a large serving bowl covered with foil in the low oven. To make the sauce pour the cream, mixed with the beaten eggs, the crushed garlic, salt and black pepper into a small saucepan. Heat very gently, stirring so that the egg makes the sauce thicken slightly, but don't boil. Mix the sauce into the noodles, add the seafood mixture, keeping some on top to look good. Serve with a crisp, green salad.

Spinach-wrapped Fish Fillets in Pastry Parcels

1 lb packet of puff pastry (450 g)
2 lb spinach – cooked and puréed with
butter and left to go cold (900 g)
3 oz grated cheese (75 g)
1¼ lb skinned, filleted white fish (560 g)
lemon juice
salt, black pepper
1 egg yolk to glaze the pastry

These golden puff pastry parcels look pretty and are exciting to eat with the layers of buttery spinach purée and tender white fish inside them. It takes a little time to wrap each one up but I find it quite fun as you can do it peacefully in advance and keep the parcels in the fridge until you want to cook them. They make a much more substantial main course than you would imagine and are best served just with a tomato salad, with bread on the side for especially hungry people. You can use any kind of fish but halibut is particularly good.

Cut the fish into six pieces, rub with lemon juice and sprinkle generously with salt and pepper. Roll out the pastry very thinly. Cut out a piece of pastry big enough to wrap up one piece of fish. Spread some cold spinach purée in the middle of the pastry, then put on a piece of fish, then spread on more spinach. Moisten the edges of the pastry with water and wrap up the fish and spinach pressing down the edges. Repeat this with the other pieces of fish. You will have to re-roll out the cut up bits of pastry several times to get pieces big enough to wrap up each bit of fish. When they are all wrapped up turn them carefully join side down on a large buttered baking sheet. Roll out the trimmings of pastry and decorate the parcels with a leaf or two. Before cooking brush the parcels all over the top with egg yolk mixed with a very little water. Bake in the centre of the oven at Gas 6 (400°F/200°C) for 25–30 minutes until golden brown. Transfer the parcels carefully with a wide flat implement on to individual plates.

Fillets of Cod in Rich Beetroot Sauce

**6 steak-size pieces of cod fillet – with
any black skin removed
salt, pepper
butter**

**FOR THE SAUCE
2 cooked beetroots – chopped up
roughly
2 oz butter (50 g)
1 inch piece of fresh root
ginger – peeled and chopped (2.5 cm)
1 tablespoon flour
1 large glass red wine
1 large glass water
juice ½ lemon
small bunch parsley – finely chopped
2–3 tablespoons cream
salt, black pepper**

I have never really liked beetroot but the colour is so beautiful that I felt I must use it somehow. I have to admit that this thick red sauce flavoured with mustard and aromatic fresh ginger goes very well with the plain cod fillets.

Salt and pepper the fish and lay it on the bottom of a buttered shallow ovenproof dish. Put a dot of butter on each slice of fish, cover dish with foil and bake in a fairly high oven Gas 6 (400°F/200°C) for 20 minutes. Meanwhile prepare the sauce.

Melt the butter in a saucepan and take off the heat. Stir the chopped beetroot and ginger into the butter and stir in the flour. Heat the wine, water and lemon juice and stir it into the saucepan with the beetroots. Bring to the boil and simmer for 3–4 minutes stirring once or twice. Whizz it up in a liquidiser or put through a Mouli until smooth. Add salt, black pepper to taste. Re-heat the sauce if necessary adding any juice from the baked fish and stir in the chopped parsley. Pour sauce all over the slices of fish and spoon over two to three tablespoons of cream before serving. I would do boiled potatoes and a fresh green vegetable with this.

Mediterranean Fish Casserole

1 lb filleted white fish (cod, haddock,
hake etc) (450 g)
1 lb squid (450 g)
½ pint fresh prawns – unpeeled (275 ml)
¾ lb cooking tomatoes (350 g)
2 pimentos (red and green if possible)
1 large clove of garlic
chicken stock
1 glass sherry
marjoram or oregano leaves (fresh if
possible)
pinch of saffron, salt, black pepper

This is a very easy dish with a nostalgic smell of summer holidays and Mediterranean harbours. You can peel the bodies of the prawns but leave the heads on for a good effect.

Pre-heat oven to Gas 6 (400°F/200°C). Cut the fish into chunks. Get the fishmonger to prepare the squid (he just takes out the ink bag and strange innards – if the extraordinary transparent bone is still there you can pull it out). Chop up the squid. Chop up the tomatoes and the pimentos. Peel and chop up the glove of garlic. Put all (except the prawns) in a casserole dish, add the saffron and sprinkle with pepper and salt. Pour over enough chicken stock just to cover. Put the lid on the dish and cook for 1–1½ hours in the centre of the oven. Ten minutes before serving add the unpeeled prawns, the sherry and the herbs. Serve with rice and a green salad.

Mussels Gratinée

5 quarts fresh mussels (5.7 litres)
1¼ pints white sauce (720 ml)
½ small glass sherry
6 oz grated cheese (175 g)
2 cloves garlic – crushed
1 level teaspoon turmeric
a little grated Parmesan – to decorate
about 2 tablespoons chopped parsley
salt, pepper
butter

This is a really delicious creamy and tasty way of serving fresh mussels either as a first course or as a light main course with a salad. You will come home from your fish shop with a shopping bag laden with mussels, but the yield is not great and to give a generous amount I think this quantity is right. It is an easy dish you can prepare well in advance and the turmeric gives it a beautiful yellow colour and subtle flavour.

Soak the mussels in cold salted water with a little flour or oatmeal thrown in, for an hour or longer if there is time. The mussels eat the flour or oatmeal and clean themselves. Scrub the mud off the mussels and pull off the seaweed-like "beard" on them. Tap any that are open, if they do not close they should be discarded. Rinse the mussels thoroughly. Put them in a large pan in about 1 in (2.5 cm) of boiling water. Cover the pan with a lid and steam the mussels open which will take 1–3 minutes. Remove the mussels from their shells and arrange them in a large fairly shallow ovenproof (earthenware looks best for this) dish. Make up about 1¼ pints (720 ml) fairly thick white sauce, season it with salt and pepper and stir into it as it simmers the grated cheese – not the Parmesan – the crushed garlic, the turmeric and the sherry. When the cheese has melted and the sauce is smooth pour it all over the mussels. Dot with butter and sprinkle with Parmesan cheese. Cook in the centre of a pre-heated oven at Gas 3 (325°F/160°C) for 30–45 minutes. To make it look extra good sprinkle some bright green chopped parsley round the edges of the dish before serving.

Souffléed Fish Pie

2 lb cod or haddock fillets – skinned
(900 g)
2 teaspoons dill or fennel seed
2–3 oz ham – chopped (50–75 g)
1 pint milk (570 ml)

about 2 oz butter (50 g)
3 tablespoons plain flour
3 oz grated cheese (75 g)
3 eggs

A large golden fish pie made with a light cheesy sauce instead of the usual mashed potato top. It is useful for a family lunch simply served with a salad and some good fresh bread.

Butter a large, fairly shallow gratinée or pie dish. Cut the fish up into pieces and lay them in the dish. Sprinkle with dill seeds, salt and pepper. Pour over the milk, cover the dish with foil and cook in a pre-heated oven at Gas 6 (400°F/200°C) for about 20 minutes. When you take the fish from the oven turn the temperature down to Gas 2 (300°F/150°C). Pour off the milk the fish has cooked in into a bowl and leave the fish in the dish. Put the chopped up ham amongst the fish. Melt about 2 oz butter in a saucepan. Remove from the heat and stir in the flour. Simmer gently for 2 minutes, stirring all the time. Gradually stir in the milk the fish was cooked in. Bring to the boil and simmer for 1 minute. Add the cheese and stir until melted and smooth. Cool slightly and then thoroughly stir in the egg yolks one by one. Check for seasoning. Whisk the egg whites until stiff and fold gently into the sauce with a metal spoon. Pour this mixture over the fish and ham and cook in the centre of the oven at Gas 2 (300°F/150°C) for about 50–60 minutes until risen and golden brown.

Stuffed Fillets of Plaice

6 small fillets of plaice (if possible
white-skinned)
1 large red pimento – chopped
oregano
2 oz peeled prawns (50 g)
1 onion – sliced finely
6 slices streaky smoked bacon, rindless
and chopped

2 oz flaked almonds (50 g)
$\frac{1}{4}$ pint single cream (150 ml)
$\frac{1}{4}$ lb button mushrooms – finely sliced
(110 g)
juice of $\frac{1}{2}$ lemon
salt, black pepper
olive oil and butter to fry in

Melt a little oil and butter in a frying pan and fry the pimento, chopped fairly small, until soft. Add the onion and chopped bacon and fry gently until just done. Transfer to a bowl. In the remaining fat gently toss the flaked almonds until golden brown. Put them into the bowl with the pimento, onion and bacon and add the prawns and a generous sprinkling of oregano, salt and black pepper. Spoon some of this mixture on each plaice fillet, fold each fillet over the stuffing, secure with a toothpick or cocktail stick and arrange in a shallow buttered fireproof dish. Cover dish with foil and cook in a fairly hot oven Gas 6 (400°F/200°C) for 25 minutes. Before serving heat up the cream (with any juices from the cooked fish) with the finely sliced mushrooms stirred into it and add salt and black pepper. Stir in the lemon juice slowly and pour the sauce over the stuffed fillets.

Smoked Mackerel Quiche

FOR THE PASTRY
10 oz plain flour (275 g)
A good pinch salt
5 oz butter (150 g)
2 oz lard (50 g)
2 oz grated cheese (50 g)
1 large egg yolk

FOR THE FILLING
1 smoked mackerel – $\frac{3}{4}$ lb in weight (350 g)
2 large onions
about $\frac{3}{4}$ pint milk (425 ml)
4 large eggs
1–2 teaspoons French mustard
salt, black pepper
1 oz butter (25 g)

A summer holiday in South Devon spent on boats and beaches has become a ritual with our family and so too have the daily picnics we take with us on our expeditions. Each morning like brushing my teeth I make the day's quiche, prick sausages ready for the beach fire and slice up Devonshire hog's pudding while the children shout and fight round me in an infuriating, restless way. But the effort is worth it for the pleasure it gives everyone to eat those delicious hot picnics in the brisk sea air. There is nothing more removed from packets of dreary sandwiches than a warm and crumbling quiche and smoky tasting sausages cooked on a driftwood fire and then wrapped in a hunk of fresh bread. Those summer holidays are one time when there is no moment to dream up food because there are too many nice outdoor things going on and hungry children running in and out of the kitchen. I rely on my standard holiday dishes which I can make without thinking. Quiches are so good for picnics and they keep really warm wrapped up in greaseproof paper and thick newspaper, even on a windy boat journey. This quiche is less usual and very delicious. If you are in a hurry don't bother to bake the pastry blind first, simply spoon in the filling and bake and it will taste very good. But if you have time the pastry is of course crisper and better if it has been baked blind.

Sift the flour and salt into a mixing bowl. Cut the butter and lard into the flour and rub with your fingertips until it is like breadcrumbs. Stir in the grated cheese with a knife and then the egg yolk and a little very cold water until the mixture just sticks together. Gather into a ball and cool in the fridge for at least half an hour. Then roll the pastry out on a floured board, and line a 9 in (23 cm) flan dish with it. If time, put the uncooked case back in the fridge for half an hour. This will help it not to shrink during the cooking. Prick the base of the pastry with a fork and bake blind, that is unfilled, in the centre of a pre-heated oven at Gas 6 (400°F/200°C) for 15 minutes.

Mix the eggs lightly with the milk, salt, pepper and mustard in a large mixing bowl. Peel and chop the onions into small pieces and fry gently in butter until soft and transparent. Stir into the mixing bowl. Take the flesh from the mackerel, discarding the skin, and flake it into the bowl. Put this mixture into the baked pastry case and bake in a pre-heated oven at Gas 5 (375°F/190°C) for 30–40 minutes until just firm in the centre. If the flan case is uncooked it may take a little longer, You can serve the quiche hot or cold but I think the pastry is so much more delicious warm. If you are making a more luxurious quiche for a party substitute cream for $\frac{1}{2}$ pint (275 ml) of the milk.

MAIN COURSE: ROASTS

Rich Glazed Joint of Brisket   page 48
Roast Juniper Veal and Special Tomato Sauce   49
Honeyed Pork with Raisins   50
Roast Leg of Lamb with Cardamom Sauce   51
Roast Saddle of Lamb with Southern Herb Sauce   52
Roast Pheasants with Curried Mushroom Sauce   53

Rich, Glazed Joint of Brisket (serves 8–10)

6–8 lb brisket on the bone fresh or salted (2.7–3.6 kg) obviously choose the leanest you can, the end bit is supposed to be the best.
1–2 teaspoons juniper berries
about 15–20 whole allspice berries
8–12 cloves
3 blades of mace – optional
3 large carrots – unscraped but roughly chopped
1 large onion – unpeeled but cut in chunks

Small bunch of any fresh herbs you can get
2–3 cooking tomatoes – cut in half
about 1 pint or slightly more red wine and stock (570 ml)
salt, black pepper
1 teaspoon mustard
2–3 teaspoons cornflour
If using salted meat –
soft brown sugar
1 cooking apple
cider – 1 pint (570 ml)

Now that one tends to buy smaller and smaller Sunday joints because of the cost it is a nice change to have a good old-fashioned hunk of meat impressively filling the carving board. Brisket is still comparatively cheap and can be dull, but cooked in the following way has a wonderful flavour. You must prepare it the day before you cook it, but the next day all you have to do is put it in the oven. You can use either fresh or salt brisket. I think the salted meat is even more delicious and has a lovely pink colour when cooked. It should be soaked in cold water for 2–3 hours before being prepared and then I rub soft brown sugar over the meat and add a cooking apple cut in chunks to the other vegetables cooked with it. Instead of wine or stock you can use cider with the salt brisket which makes a specially good combination of flavours for the gravy. When you serve this generous piece of meat, shining and aromatic, it really will bring cheer to a bleak winter weekend.

Trim any thick fat from the meat. Rub all over with salt and black pepper, and put the joint into either a very large casserole or a roasting pan. Roughly crush the juniper berries and allspice and put them in the casserole with the carrots, onion, tomatoes, cloves, mace and the meat. Pour over the wine mixture. Cover as hermetically as possible with foil or a lid and leave at normal room temperature overnight. The next day put the covered dish in a low oven Gas 2 (300°F/150°C) and cook for 5–5½ hours, basting occasionally. Then lift the joint out on to a carving board and strain off the juices from which you should pour off quite a lot of fat, which will make very good dripping. Put just a little juice in a saucepan and boil fiercely until it reduces to a thick glaze – brush the meat all over with this. Blend the cornflour with a little cold water, stir it into the remaining juices with the mustard and bring to the boil. Bubble for a minute or two and serve as a very delicious gravy. Carve the joint in fairly thick chunks.

Roast Juniper Veal and Special Tomato Sauce

1 joint of veal on the bone – about 4 lb
would do for 6 people (1.8 kg)
olive oil
juice of 1 lemon
2–3 cloves of garlic – chopped small
about a dessertspoon of juniper
berries – crushed
salt and black pepper

FOR THE SAUCE
2–3 glasses of red wine
½ lb tomatoes dipped in boiling water,
skinned and chopped up small (225 g)
1 teaspoon Marmite or Bovril dissolved
in a cup of hot water
2 teaspoons mild French mustard,
preferably the whole seed type
juices from the meat
1 dessertspoon cornflour
salt, black pepper

You need not choose the very expensive Dutch veal for this – you can use the smaller English kind which is sometimes quite cheap. The gravy is the important thing and can make an ordinary Sunday joint really special. If possible, prepare the meat for roasting for several hours or even the day before you cook it.

Make deep incisions in the meat and poke the crushed juniper berries and the chopped garlic in as far as you can. In a cup mix the lemon juice and about twice the amount of olive oil – if you have a garlic crusher add a small clove of crushed garlic, salt and black pepper. Rub this mixture all over the meat. Put the meat in a roasting pan spooning any extra mixture over the meat. Cover the pan with foil and leave in a cool place for several hours. Once or twice spoon any juice which has slipped off the meat over it again. Allow about 35–40 minutes per pound to cook. Pre-heat the oven to Gas 4 (350°F/180°C) and cook the meat, still covered with foil, in the centre of the oven. Half an hour before serving, take off the foil, baste the meat and continue to cook uncovered. Begin making the gravy about 30 minutes before the meat is ready to serve. Gently simmer the chopped tomatoes in the wine for about 15–20 minutes. Then stir in the Marmite water and the mustard, salt and black pepper and any juices from the roasting meat. Mix the cornflour with a little extra wine to a smooth paste. Stir in a little tomato mixture and then mix this into the main bulk of the sauce, bring to the boil and simmer for 2–3 minutes. If it seems too thick add a little wine or water. Put in a jug and serve with the joint.

Honeyed Pork with Raisins

2–3 lb joint of pork (900 g–1.35 kg)
1–2 sprigs rosemary
raisins
honey
1 15-oz tin tomatoes (425 g)
1 wineglass cider or wine (or a small
glass of sherry)
salt, black pepper

As with most joints to be roasted I try to leave this overnight at room temperature rubbed with its flavourings. A boneless joint with any thick skin taken off is best for this recipe. The honey seems to make the meat succulent and mellow, and the tomato mixed with the pan juices is delicious.

Make deep incisions in the meat with a sharp thin knife and press in raisins and rosemary leaves with your fingers. Salt and pepper the joint and then smear liberally with honey all over. Put into a greased roasting dish and leave in a cool place, but not the fridge, for 12 hours or overnight. Baste the meat with the honey juice. Cook in the centre of the oven at Gas 3 (325°F/160°C) for about 1½ hours. Mush up the contents of a tin of tomatoes with a fork or a liquidiser, and mix with the cider, salt and black pepper. Pour off excess fat from the roasting pan. Add the tomatoes and cider and continue cooking the meat for another half an hour. Carve the joint thickly and use the juices as a sauce.

Roast Leg of Lamb with Cardamom Sauce

1 leg of lamb (preferably English, or
best of all Welsh)
about 8 cardamom pods
juice of ½ lemon
1 tablespoon of olive oil
1 oz butter (25 g)
1 oz cornflour (25 g)
¾ pint milk (425 ml)
2 teaspoons mild French mustard (the
very mild whole seed kind is best)
1 dessertspoon of powdered cardamom
(you should be able to get this and
the whole kind at delicatessens
or Indian grocers)
salt, black pepper

This is really just a very delicious sauce to make a Sunday joint more exciting. I have put down quantities for a generous amount of sauce as it always seems to be very lavishly used on the meat.

Several hours or the day before you roast it make several incisions in the lamb. Peel the cardamom pods and find several little black seeds inside. Stick these into the incisions in the lamb. Put the lamb on a dish and rub all over with a mixture of the olive oil, lemon juice, salt and black pepper. Leave in a coolish place (not in the fridge). Then pre-heat the oven to Gas 5 (375°F/190°C). Rub a bit more olive oil over the lamb and roast for about 2 hours, basting occasionally (the time may vary according to the size of the leg – I am assuming one weighing 4–5 lb (1.75–2.25 kg). Now make the sauce. Start by melting the butter and take off the heat. Stir in the cornflour then fairly gradually add the milk. Put back on the heat, bring to the boil stirring continuously (when it will thicken) and simmer for 3 minutes gently. Stir in the mustard, the powdered cardamom and salt and black pepper to taste. When the joint is ready, pour off the excess fat from the baking pan and stir the remaining juices into the sauce. Put the sauce into a gravy jug and serve with the lamb. New or boiled potatoes go much better with this sauce than roast ones.

Roast Saddle of Lamb with Southern Herb Sauce

(serves 8–12)

1 saddle English or Welsh lamb
1 lemon
1 clove of garlic – crushed
about 1 tablespoon thyme
leaves – fresh if possible
about 1 tablespoon oregano leaves
salt, black pepper
olive oil

FOR THE SAUCE
1 oz butter (25 g)
1 oz cornflower (25 g)
½ pint milk (275 ml)
1 egg yolk
1 tablespoon thyme leaves
1 tablespoon oregano leaves
1 glove garlic – crushed
juices from the meat

A saddle of English or Welsh lamb for a large dinner party is so easy to do and yet always impressive and very delicious. My husband maintains that the French way of carving it in long thin strips down the length of the joint instead of across is much the best. A saddle can feed up to about 12 people but I usually do one for 8 or 10 and we have scraps of meat left over for the children next day. This is a way of roasting and flavouring a saddle which is meant to bring to you the smell and feeling of those dry hillsides in Greece and the South of France where thyme and oregano grow wild among the bright flowering cistus.

Prepare the joint in advance. Put the lamb in a roasting pan. Squeeze the juice from the lemon, reserving the lemon skin. Mix the juice with a little olive oil, the garlic, salt and black pepper. Rub the lamb all over with this mixture. Sprinkle the herbs on the underside and in any cracks. Rub the top of the joint with a little olive oil and salt. Cut the lemon skin up roughly into quarters and place the pieces on the underside of the joint. Cover the pan with a cloth and leave at room temperature for several hours or overnight. Heat the oven to Gas 4 (350°F/180°C) and roast the joint in the centre of the oven for about 20–25 minutes per pound basting occasionally.

Melt the butter in a saucepan. Remove from the heat and blend in the cornflour. Stir in ½ pint milk (275 ml) and bring to the boil, stirring. Season with salt, black pepper, the crushed garlic and the herbs. Simmer gently for 2–3 minutes. When the meat is done pour off the excess fat and stir the remaining juices into the sauce. Remove from the heat and thoroughly stir in the egg yolk before serving with the roast meat.

Roast Pheasants with Curried Mushroom Sauce

2 pheasants
3 tablespoons oil
2 tablespoons tomato purée
2 teaspoons powdered cumin
3 teaspoons curry powder
2 teaspoons powdered coriander
1 teaspoon powdered cardamom
1 tablespoon wine vinegar
1 lemon and juice of 1 orange

FOR THE SAUCE
½ lb mushrooms – sliced crossways (225 g)
butter, oil
1 heaped tablespoon plain flour
2 large tomatoes – skinned and chopped

2–3 teaspoons curry powder – to taste
2 teaspoons powdered cumin
2 teaspoons powdered coriander
2 teaspoons powdered cardamom
2 teaspoons ground ginger
1 teaspoon turmeric
1 tablespoon tomato purée
juice of ½ large or 1 small lemon
2 heaped tablespoons creamed coconut – you can buy this in cartons made by Mapletons – it thickens and improves the consistency of curries

This makes a delicious change with pheasants and the rich mushroom sauce is particularly good. It is really worth using all the different spices in the curry and they are very useful to have for all sorts of things, and for several of the dishes in this book. Again, I recommend well-buttered Basmati rice with this.

Put the oil, tomato purée, vinegar and all the spices into a small bowl and mix thoroughly. Brush this mixture all over the birds. Put them in a covered ovenproof dish, pour the orange juice into the dish and if possible, leave for several hours or overnight at room temperature. Then put into the middle of a moderate to low oven Gas 3 (325°F/160°C) for 1½–2 hours, basting occasionally. Meanwhile make the mushroom curry sauce to serve with the birds.

Melt a tablespoonful of olive oil with 1 oz butter (25 g) in a fairly large saucepan. Remove from heat and stir in the sliced mushrooms and chopped tomatoes. Stir in the flour. Add a mixture of 1 tablespoonful tomato purée mixed with 1 pint water (570 ml). Add all the spices and the salt and stir in the lemon juice and the creamed coconut – this melts very quickly into the hot sauce. Bring to the boil, stirring often – then simmer for 10 minutes. Taste and add any curry or spices if necessary. If the sauce looks very thick add a little bit of milk. Transfer to a serving bowl, cover and keep warm in a very low oven until you are ready to serve the pheasants. Put the pheasants on a carving board. I usually put a small ladle into the bowl of sauce so people can pour it over the pheasant on their plates. Serve with rice and green salad or a bright green vegetable like broccoli.

MAIN COURSE: CASSEROLES

Braised Steak in Sherry with Mushrooms   page 56
Hearty Beef Casserole   57
Delicious Veal and Prune Curry   58
Dittisham Casserole   59
Lamb Fillets with Mint   59
Joints of Chicken Baked with Cinnamon   60
Creamy Blanquette of Rabbit with Mustard   61

Braised Steak in Sherry with Mushrooms

1¾–2 lb stewing steak (800–900 g) –
ask your butcher to cut it in large
pieces like thick rump steaks
¾ lb mushrooms – sliced (350 g)
10–12 sage leaves – chopped and
fresh if possible
¼ pint soured cream (150 ml)
2 large cloves garlic
1 small glass dry sherry
about ½ a small glass olive oil
salt, black pepper

This is a way to use stewing steak which makes it look and taste much grander than an ordinary stew. The meat is cooked slowly in the sherry and served with a topping of lightly done mushrooms. It is very simple to prepare, but do it in advance so that the meat can marinate.

Rub the pieces of steak all over with crushed garlic (use a garlic crusher). Then pepper with a generous amount of black pepper and arrange the meat in a large shallow gratinée dish. Mix the sherry and olive oil and a little salt together with a fork and pour the mixture over the meat. Cover dish with foil and leave at room temperature for several hours, turning meat once or twice. Cook, still covered with foil in a low oven Gas 2 (300°F/150°C) for about 2–2½ hours until meat is tender. Pour the juice from the dish into a frying pan and cook the mushrooms and sage in the juice for just 2–3 minutes. Arrange the mushrooms and sage on top of the pieces of steak. Bubble any remaining juice in the pan over a fierce heat until reduced and thicker. Pour over the meat. Lastly spoon the soured cream in dollops over the top and serve. Baked potatoes are very good with this and a fresh green vegetable or very young carrots.

Hearty Beef Casserole

½ lb ox heart (225 g)
1 lb stewing beef (450 g)
½ lb smoked streaky bacon — thickly
sliced and roughly chopped (225 g)
2 tablespoons plain flour
about ¾ pint stock (425 ml) made from
mixing and heating together 1 glass of
red wine, ½ pint beef stock (275 ml),
a sprinkling of Worcestershire sauce,
black pepper and salt to taste
½ lb carrots — peeled and chopped
(225 g)
1 onion — peeled and chopped
4 cooking tomatoes — chopped
few coriander seeds ⎫ crushed
about 8 juniper berries ⎬ together in
a few allspice berries ⎭ a mortar
2–3 cardamom pods — roughly crushed
a little oil and butter for pan

People usually hate the idea of heart but this is a rich and strongly flavoured dish, good for winter weekend lunches or suppers. It is the heart which gives the rich flavour, but if you think your family will refuse to eat it, don't tell them about the heart. They will never know.

Chop beef and heart into cubes. (Discard any tubes in the heart.) Melt enough oil and butter to thickly cover the bottom of an iron casserole dish. Stir the beef, heart and bacon into the fat. Stir in the flour. Add the heated stock and stir. Bring gently to the boil until it thickens. Take off the heat and add the chopped carrots, the onion and tomatoes and the crushed spices. Put back on the heat and bring to simmering point. Cover dish and put in a low oven Gas 1 (275°F/140°C) for 3½–4 hours. Serve with boiled long grain rice and a green vegetable or salad.

Delicious Veal and Prune Curry

FOR THE MARINADE
juice of 1 orange
1 tablespoon wine vinegar
2–3 tablespoons oil

FOR THE CURRY
4–6 oz prunes – soaked overnight
(110–175 g)
2 lb stewing veal (900 g)
pinch of mustard seeds
1 heaped teaspoon whole
coriander seeds
1 heaped teaspoon cumin
seeds
pinch fenugreek seeds
5–10 cardamom pods – roughly
crushed

} Ground in a blender or pounded in a mortar

2 large cloves garlic – chopped
2 small pieces cinnamon bark
1–2 slices green ginger – chopped
finely. (This is available in good
greengrocers and markets as well
as in Indian shops.)
a few curry leaves if
available – chopped
1 teaspoon powdered turmeric
½–1 teaspoon powdered chilli
1 dessertspoon soft brown sugar
1–2 heaped tablespoons creamed
coconut
½ pint yoghurt (275 ml)
chopped mint leaves, chives or parsley
salt

It is very satisfying to make a real curry without just throwing in a teaspoon of stale curry powder which always has the same taste. Getting together your own spices is more trouble but the result is quite different and far better, and I think well worth the little extra time and trouble. This fairly mild curry has a really delicious, creamy but fresh flavour and you can get the right spices for it from an Indian shop, a delicatessen or even a large supermarket. Of course if you cannot get one or two of the ingredients do not worry, just put in what you can and I am sure you will be pleased with the result. You do not have to marinate the meat but I think it makes it much better.

Marinate the meat and soak the prunes overnight. Then get all your spices together ready prepared before you start the curry. Melt a large knob of butter and a tablespoon of oil in a large pan (or cast-iron casserole dish which you can also use to cook the curry in) and gently fry the ground spices, the chopped ginger, the crushed cardamom pods and the curry leaves. Stir in the meat, the turmeric, the chilli powder, the brown sugar, the garlic and the pieces of cinnamon. If you are not already using a cast-iron dish transfer the meat mixture to a casserole dish and pour over ¼–½ pint of stock or water (150–275 ml) – the liquid should almost cover the meat. Add salt to taste. Heat to simmering point either on top of the stove or in a high oven and then cook gently in the middle of the oven at Gas 1–2 (275°–300°F/140°–150°C) for 1½ hours or until the meat is tender. Stone the soaked prunes and add them to the curry. Stir in the creamed coconut which will thicken the juice and make it taste more delicious, and lastly add the yoghurt. If it seems to have gone too cold re-heat briefly, or you can keep it warm in a very low oven until you are ready to eat it. Finally sprinkle the chopped mint leaves or other greenery on top of the curry and serve with Basmati rice and a crisp salad.

Dittisham Casserole

2 lb lean stewing pork or pork
fillet – cut up in chunks (900 g)
1 level teaspoon whole coriander seeds
sprig of rosemary – fresh if possible
2 onions – peeled and sliced

4 oz mushrooms sliced (110 g)
2 cooking apples – peeled, cored and
cut up into chunks
juice of ½ lemon
about 1 large wineglass of strong, dry
cider

Summer-holiday cooking has to be quick and simple and able to be prepared in advance, but with all the outdoor life people's appetites are keen so things must taste good. On our yearly Devon holiday I find this easy casserole of pork cooked in the local cider especially appetising. "Scrumpy" is a draught cider, strong and very dry though if you cannot get it just substitute a good dry cider.

Fry the pork and sliced onions in a little fat briefly until just browned. Put them in a casserole dish. Add the rosemary, coriander, salt and pepper. Pour over the cider and lemon juice which should nearly cover the meat – if it does not, add more cider. Cover the dish and cook in the centre of a high oven Gas 7–8 (425°–450°F/220°–230°C) for 15 minutes then turn down low to Gas 1–2 (275°–300°F/140°–150°C) for 1½–2 hours. About ½ hour before it has finished cooking add the sliced mushrooms and chunks of apple. I think it is good served with baked potatoes and small whole carrots.

Lamb Fillets with Mint

2 lb lamb neck fillets (900 g)
good handful fresh mint
leaves – roughly chopped
about 1 pint stock (570 ml)
1 tablespoon plain flour

olive oil
butter
2 teaspoons powdered cumin
pine nuts (optional)

This is a very good summer casserole and has a Middle Eastern flavour. Some pine nuts toasted in butter and added at the last moment make it even better. It is good with new potatoes and fresh peas or just a tomato salad.

Cut meat up into pieces. Melt a little butter and olive oil in a metal or iron casserole. Turn off heat and toss the meat in the melted oil and butter. Stir in the flour and gradually add enough hot stock to cover the meat. Bring to the boil until it has thickened. Add salt, black pepper, about 2 teaspoons of powdered cumin, the roughly chopped up mint, and simmer in a moderate oven Gas 3–4 (325°–350°F/160°–180°C) for about 1½ hours. Just before serving, add the pine nuts toasted in butter until golden brown.

Joints of Chicken Baked with Cinnamon

6 pieces of chicken
2 cloves garlic – crushed
3–4 tomatoes
1 orange – sliced in rounds
1 lemon – sliced in rounds
stick cinnamon
handful of black olives – stoned and
halved
1 glass white wine or sherry
olive oil
salt, black pepper

On an island in the Aegean, in the middle of an olive grove, my husband's prep school headmaster has built himself his life's dream – a small, square, whitewashed tower with arched windows and pilasters round the top where, in his retirement, he goes for most of the year to paint. One summer just after we married we decided to visit him there; the bus dropped us at a café on the beach and we stumbled towards his tower with our suitcases through the stubbly grass of the olive groves. We had a happy time but, living alone, his diet seemed to consist of bread and a bumper jar of Marmite from England. So I cooked a bit and there wrote my first recipe; a simple stew which he could do for himself if he tired of the Marmite. I also learnt from a restaurant in the town how to cook chicken in the easiest and most delicious way, flavoured with stick cinnamon. They told me it was a common way to cook chicken in Greece but I have never had it like that again. Here is the way that I do it.

Pre-heat the oven to Gas 5 (375°F/190°C). Smear the pieces of chicken all over with the crushed garlic, sprinkle with salt and pepper. Brush each piece of chicken with olive oil and put in a wide, fairly shallow ovenproof serving dish. Put 6–10 pieces of stick cinnamon over and under the chicken. Slice up the tomatoes and arrange them with the olives around the pieces of chicken. Put a round slice of lemon and orange on each piece of chicken. Pour over the wine, cover the dish with foil and bake in the centre of the oven for an hour. This dish is very good with buttered noodles instead of potatoes.

Creamy Blanquette of Rabbit with Mustard

1½ lb boned rabbit or about 2 lb chopped
rabbit on the bone (700 or 900 g)
2 tablespoons plain flour
½–¾ pint milk (275–425 ml)
butter and oil for the pan
8 fluid oz single cream (225 ml)
2 egg yolks
juice of ½ lemon
1 dessertspoon of honey
4–5 teaspoons Moutarde de Meaux (or
other mild preferably whole seed
French mustard)
6–8 juniper berries – crushed
½ lb small mushrooms (225 g)
salt, black pepper

You can usually buy frozen boneless rabbit at Sainsbury's and some butchers, and it is very useful for this dish. If you can't get it just use rabbit from your butcher chopped up into fairly small pieces – but the boneless rabbit makes it more like a real blanquette.

Melt about 1 oz of butter (25 g) and a little oil (enough to coat the pieces of rabbit) in an iron casserole on top of the stove. Put in the rabbit and stir. Take off the heat and stir in the flour. Heat the milk, seasoned with salt and black pepper and pour on to the rabbit. Stir well. Put on the heat again and bring to the boil stirring frequently until it thickens. Take off the heat and add the crushed juniper berries, the mustard and the honey. Taste and add more mustard if you want it stronger. Bring up to simmering point once more and put in a pre-heated oven Gas 3 (325°F/160°C) for about 1½ hours. Slice the mushrooms in fine slices sideways (so they make a nice mushroom shape). Whisk the egg yolks into the cream with a fork. Stir the lemon juice into the rabbit, then the cream and egg yolks, and lastly the mushrooms (these should only get warm in the mixture not cooked). Check for seasoning and slightly re-heat on top of the stove if it has gone cool but do not boil. Serve with new potatoes or long grain rice and either a green salad or a very fresh green vegetable, or baby carrots if it is the right time of year for them.

MAIN COURSE: PIES

Special Shepherd's Pie   page 64
Oriental Pie   65
Ratatouille in a Veal Case   66
Stuffed Veal in a Pastry Case   67
Stuffed Boned Chicken en Croûte   68
Chicken Coriander Pie with Cider and Mustard   69
Pigeon Pie   70
Kidney Layer Pie   71

Special Shepherd's Pie

1½–2 lb minced beef or lamb (700–
900 g)
1–2 large onions – peeled and chopped
2 teaspoons powdered cumin
1 small tin of tomatoes
1–2 tablespoons roughly chopped sage
leaves – fresh if possible
1½–2 lb mashed potatoes with plenty of
butter and milk added (700–900 g)
3 oz grated cheese (75 g)
2 eggs
a little grated Parmesan

This is just a very good tasting shepherd's pie with a slightly more interesting top than the usual dry mash. I think it is ideal for family Saturday lunch with salad, and it is useful to make it beforehand so that the weekend is more relaxed. Of course fresh potatoes are best for the top mixture but it is so disguised by egg and cheese that you can use instant mash if you are in a rush!

Fry the chopped onions gently and put on one side. Sprinkle the mince with the powdered cumin and plenty of salt and pepper and fry it in a little fat in a large deep frying pan, digging at it with a wooden spoon to separate it. When it is all separate, add the onions, the chopped sage and the tin of tomatoes and mix it with the meat. Transfer to a large, preferably rather shallow ovenproof dish. Heat oven to Gas 3–4 (325°–350°F/ 160°–180°C). Lightly beat the two eggs and add them with the grated cheese and some black pepper to the mashed potatoes which should be made less firm than usual by adding more milk. Cover the meat with this mixture then sprinkle the top with grated Parmesan and put in the oven until the top is risen and golden brown (about 1 hour or a bit more). Serve with a green salad.

Oriental Pie

1¾ lb minced beef (800 g)
3–4 teaspoons kabab paste or curry
paste (these useful concoctions are
sold in Indian grocers or delicatessens
in jars)
or 2–3 teaspoons curry powder
2 tablespoons tomato purée
1 teaspoon powdered cumin
½ lb spinach leaves – chopped small
(225 g)
1 large swede, weighing 1–1½ lb –
boiled and mashed with butter and
black pepper (450–700 g)
2 eggs – beaten
sesame seeds (optional)
salt, pepper

I'm sure there is nothing like shepherd's pie in India but this dish is a mixture of shepherd's pie and Greek moussaka with an Indian flavour, which goes well with the slight sweetness of the swede topping.

In a bowl mix up the mince with the kabab paste or the curry powder, cumin, salt and two tablespoons tomato purée. Fry the mixture over a high heat in a little oil digging at it with a wooden spoon to keep it separate. Taste, add more paste or powder if you like things hot. If it tastes too hot add some lemon juice to it. Put the mixture in a large shallow ovenproof dish and pat down. Put the chopped spinach on the meat and pat down. Mix the mashed swede with the beaten eggs and put on top. Sprinkle with sesame seeds and dot with butter. Put in a moderate oven Gas 3 (325°F/160°C) for about an hour until it is golden brown on top. Serve with a salad.

Ratatouille in a Veal Case

FOR THE FILLING
¾ lb tomatoes (350 g)
½ lb mushrooms (225 g)
2 green peppers
1 large onion
olive oil
butter
salt, pepper

FOR THE MEAT CASE
1½ lb minced veal (700 g)
1 tablespoon tomato purée
about 1 tablespoon chopped rosemary
2 cloves garlic – crushed
3 teaspoons French mustard
2 small or 1 large egg – lightly whisked
3 oz plain flour – wholemeal tastes
good for this (75 g)
salt, black pepper

Mince is so versatile but really needs imaginative seasoning and many people say they don't know what to do with it beyond shepherd's pie. This is a sort of ratatouille (you can alter the vegetables if you like, according to what you have) in a minced veal case flavoured with tomato, garlic, mustard and rosemary. I have it as a main course with fried potatoes and a simple green salad, and it is unusual and very good. You can ask the butcher to mince some pie veal for you. Large supermarkets now often sell minced veal, or pork which you could also use for this recipe.

Make the filling first. Melt a little olive oil and butter in a large frying pan. Chop up the peppers and onions and gently fry them until they have softened. Then chop up the tomatoes – I think they are better skinned – and the mushrooms and add them to the onions and peppers. Let mixture cool in the pan while you prepare the meat case.

FOR THE MEAT CASE

Heat oven to Gas 3 (325°F/160°C). In a mixing bowl put the veal, the rosemary, the crushed garlic, the mustard, the tomato purée, a very generous sprinkling of salt and black pepper and the whisked egg. Mix all thoroughly together with a wooden spoon. Stir in the flour. Flour a board. Have ready an 8–9 in (20–23 cm) flan dish – a china or earthenware one is best for this. With floured hands gather the mixture up into a ball. Take just under two thirds of it and press it out with your floured hands on to the board in a circular shape bigger than the flan dish. Line the flan dish with the circle, pushing it up the sides so it extends slightly over the rim. Put the vegetable filling in. Now make another flat circle with the remaining meat mixture, moisten the edge with a little water and put it on top, pressing down the edges so that they overlap a bit as the meat will shrink slightly while cooking. Spoon or brush a little olive oil over the top. Bake in the centre of the oven for ¾–1 hour. To serve just cut it in slices like a pie.

Stuffed Veal in a Pastry Case

FOR THE STUFFING
4–5 oz fresh white breadcrumbs
(110–150 g)
about 1 oz butter (25 g)
a good handful of sage leaves – finely
chopped
3–4 oz grated cheese (75–110 g)
3 cloves garlic – crushed
a very little milk
salt, black pepper

OTHER INGREDIENTS
2–3 lb piece of boneless veal
(900 g–1.35 kg)
2 cloves garlic – crushed
juice of $\frac{1}{2}$ lemon
12 oz–1 lb packet puff pastry (more if
you get a larger piece of meat) (350–
450 g)
1 egg yolk
olive oil
salt, pepper

I think a shiny golden pastry parcel of succulent meat is both delicious and beautiful, and very exciting when you cut through the crisp case to reveal the meat and perhaps a stuffing too. The best way to do it is to cook the meat in advance, (use boned lamb if you cannot get veal) cool it and then wrap the pastry round and put in the oven again for as long as it takes to cook the pastry until it is golden brown. This stops the meat shrinking from the pastry which also will not be hard and overcooked. For this recipe you can use the cheaper breast of veal if you like, shoulder or loin. Ask the butcher to bone it but not to roll it. As it is done in stages, you must start this recipe well in advance, but the final cooking is completely simple and quick.

Make up the stuffing by roughly rubbing the butter into the breadcrumbs in a bowl and then stirring in the sage, the grated cheese and crushed garlic. Season with salt and pepper and stir in a little cold milk until the mixture just sticks together. Lay the piece of meat out and put the stuffing in the middle of it. Now roll the meat over the stuffing and tie it with string (skewers too if it helps) into as neat a parcel as you can. Do not worry about having a lot of string as you will remove it before wrapping the pastry round the joint. Mix together with a fork the lemon juice and about 2 tablespoons of olive oil, adding the crushed garlic, salt and pepper. Put the meat into a roasting pan and rub this mixture all over it. Cover with a cloth and leave at room temperature for several hours, or overnight, turning the joint in the oil and lemon mixture occasionally. Then remove the cloth and cook in the centre of the oven at Gas 4 (350°F/180°C) for about 30 minutes per pound, basting occasionally. Remove the joint from the pan. Drain excess fat from the pan but reserve any meat juices. Cool the meat down completely and then cut away the string. When the meat is cold roll out the pastry thinly to a size big enough to envelop the meat. Moisten the edges of the pastry and wrap it round the meat, cutting off the end bits so as not to make thick fold-overs. Place the roll in a baking tray with the joins underneath. Roll out the trimmings and decorate the parcel with leaves, etc. I enjoy this and have even decorated this joint with a pastry calf munching grass under a tree! If you do not want to cook it immediately, put it in the fridge. Otherwise, brush it with egg yolk and bake in the centre of a pre-heated oven Gas 6 (400°F/200°C) for 40–45 minutes. If it looks as if it is getting too brown put a piece of foil on top. I usually serve it with a creamy sauce made by mixing the reserved meat juices with a carton of single cream, salt and pepper to taste, and a very little lemon juice and heating it gently, taking care not to boil it.

Stuffed Boned Chicken en Croûte

1 boned chicken
¼ lb mushrooms (110 g)
tarragon (fresh if possible)
1 crushed clove of garlic
salt, pepper
8–12 oz packet of bought puff pastry or
short pastry (225–350 g)
string and skewers
juice of 1 lemon for the gravy
little white wine
1 egg yolk

You can really only do this if you are prepared to bone a chicken or can find a butcher who will bone one for you – in the country they often will and do not charge anything, and good London butchers usually will if they like you! It is a very pretty, impressive dinner party dish, fairly easy, but it has to be done in two stages so start in time or do the first part well ahead to make it easier later when you are busy.

Heat oven to Gas 5–6 (375°–400°F/190°–200°C). The butcher will probably give you a shapeless mass of chicken, though occasionally it is done perfectly and is still in chicken shape. Lay it out flat and rub the inside with the crushed garlic. Sprinkle with salt and pepper. In the middle put a pile of sliced mushrooms and chopped tarragon. Now it is like tying up a difficult parcel. Wrap the chicken round the mushrooms and tie it up with string as neatly as possible with no mushrooms popping out – it does not matter how much string or how many skewers you use because they all come off later. Put the bundle, rubbed with olive oil, into a roasting pan in the oven for ¾ hour. Take it out and let it get cold (save the pan juices to use as a sauce or gravy later). Remove the string and skewers when it is cold. About half an hour before your meal, heat oven to Gas 7 (425°F/220°C). Roll out the pastry and wrap it round the lump of chicken making sure the joins are underneath. If you have time and artistic inspiration use the left-over pastry to make little cut out leaves and flowers or any kind of patterns you like. Brush with egg yolk and put the parcel in the oven for about 20 minutes until the pastry looks cooked and golden.

TO SERVE, cut in slices with a very sharp knife. Any nice fresh vegetables will go with this. For the gravy add the juice of ½ a lemon and a little white wine to the pan juices and re-heat, having taken off any excess fat.

Chicken Coriander Pie with Cider and Mustard

FOR THE PASTRY
12 oz "strong" flour – usually used for
bread making (350 g)
½ teaspoon salt
6 oz butter or margarine (175 g)
3 oz lard (75 g)
a little cold water
FOR THE PIE FILLING
1¼ lb boneless chicken (660 g) – your
butcher might bone you some chicken
or you can buy boneless chicken at
Sainsbury's or Marks and Spencer

1 large cooking apple – peeled, cored
and cut in chunks
2 large carrots – cut in rounds
2 onions – peeled and cut up fairly small
¼ lb mushrooms – sliced (110 g)
3 heaped tablespoons flour
just over 1 pint dry cider (570 ml)
3 teaspoons powdered coriander
3 teaspoons mild French mustard
¼ pint soured cream (150 ml)
olive oil, butter
salt, black pepper

I make this pie in a round china flan dish and then everyone gets a good slice of the rich and crumbly pastry. The combination of flavours in the filling is delicious and the pie is very good eaten hot or cold for lunch or dinner, or you could make a larger version for a cold buffet. If you have it cold serve it at room temperature, not straight from the fridge. I do not think it needs potatoes with it, just a green salad. You can make the pie well in advance, so with no vegetables to do it is a very peaceful meal to serve.

Cut the fat into the flour and salt in a mixing bowl. Rub with your fingertips until the mixture resembles breadcrumbs. Stir in a very little cold water – if you have any iced water in the fridge all the better – until the mixture only just begins to stick together. Gather up into a ball and leave in the fridge for at least half an hour, or until the next day if you like.

Heat oven to Gas 4 (350°F/180°C). Melt a little olive oil and 1–2oz butter in an iron casserole dish on top of the stove and remove from the heat. (If you haven't got an iron casserole do it in a large frying pan and transfer later to an ordinary casserole dish.) Cut the chicken up into fairly small pieces. Stir the chicken and the sliced onions and carrots into the melted fat in the casserole. Stir in the flour. Meanwhile heat the cider and stir it into the chicken mixture. Add salt and pepper, the coriander and the mustard. Bring to the boil, stirring once or twice and when it thickens and is simmering cover the dish and cook in the centre of the oven at Gas 4 (350°F/180°C) for ¾ hour, stirring it once during the cooking. Take out and add the chopped apple and sliced mushrooms and then return the covered dish to the oven for a further 10 minutes. It should be a thick and creamy casserole – if it looks too thin at the end blend a little more flour with some water and add it to the stew. Then bring to the boil and simmer, stirring, for 3 minutes. Stir the soured cream into the casserole, check for seasoning and pour the mixture into a large shallow dish – I use a china flan dish about 9–10 in (23–25.5 cm) diameter, 1½ in (4 cm) deep. Let cool. Roll out the pastry fairly thickly, roughly the size and shape of your dish. Dampen the edges of the dish. Roll the pastry back over the rolling pin and out again on to the dish. Trim the edges of the pastry very slightly larger than the dish and then press down the edges lightly. Roll out the scraps of pastry and use to decorate as you like. For a special occasion the pie will look really professional and beautiful if you take time doing the decoration and glaze it by brushing all over with an egg yolk. Heat the oven to Gas 6 (400°F/200°C) and bake just about the centre for 25–30 minutes until golden brown.

Pigeon Pie

4 wood pigeons
¾ lb pigs' kidney (350 g)
½ lb carrots – sliced (225 g)
2 oz rindless streaky bacon, sliced
small and chopped (50 g)
2 large peeled tomatoes
1 dessertspoon oregano
about 12 crushed coriander seeds
2 glasses red wine
about 1 pint stock, preferably made
from the pigeon carcasses (570 ml)
2 tablespoons plain flour
salt, pepper
1 packet puff pastry (or short pastry)

You can make the filling of the pie well in advance so that the final cooking time is just about 20 minutes to cook the pastry. If you can't get fresh pigeons Sainsbury's nearly always sell frozen ones which can be used for this delicious gamy pie.

Cut as much pigeon meat as you can from the bones (you can use the carcasses to boil up with bay leaf, onion, salt and black peppercorns to make a delicious stock) and roughly cut up. Slice the pigs' kidney, the bacon and the carrots. Melt a mixture of 1 tablespoon of oil and 1–2 oz of butter (25–50 g) in the bottom of a large heavy pan. Put the pigeon, kidney and bacon in and toss in the fat but do not brown. Take off heat and stir in the flour. Add heated red wine and enough stock to cover the meat. Put on heat and bring to simmering point until it thickens, stirring often. If it is too thick add more stock. Stir in the carrots, tomatoes and oregano, coriander seeds, salt and black pepper. Bring to the boil and transfer to a hot pie dish which the mixture fills to the top. Cover with foil and cook in the centre of a pre-heated oven Gas 4 (350°F/180°C) for about 1½ hours. Take out and cool. Roll out the pastry fairly thickly and big enough to cover the top of the pie dish. Dampen the rim of the pie dish and carefully lay on the pastry. Press down the edges and cut off neatly. Roll out the scraps and cut out some decorations. These can be as elaborate or as simple as you feel inclined. I really enjoy doing leaves, flowers, birds, even animals. I sometimes cut out letters for messages if it is someone's birthday or a special occasion – or I have just written "Bon appetit"! Brush the pastry with some egg yolk (this makes it look so much grander; shiny, golden and professional). Pre-heat oven to Gas 6 (400°F/200°C) and cook pie for about 20 minutes until the pastry looks just right. I don't think you need potatoes with pies, just some carefully cooked fresh green vegetables.

Kidney Layer Pie

2½ lb mashed potatoes, seasoned and
buttered (a generous kg)
1 large egg (or 2 small) – lightly
whisked
2 large onions
1 oz butter (25 g)
1 tablespoon oil
10 lambs' kidneys
4–6 tomatoes (depending on
size) – cut up into eighths
1 dessertspoon oregano, thyme or
rosemary
2 cloves garlic – finely chopped
8 oz grated cheese (225 g)
salt, black pepper

*This is a good dish for Saturday lunch as both adults and children enjoy it and even though
it is fairly quick to do you can prepare it the day before if you are going to have a busy
weekend. The flavours seep into the mashed potato and are delicious. You just need a
simple green salad with it. This amount will probably feed four hungry adults and three
children.*

Let the mashed potatoes cool a bit and then stir the whisked egg in thoroughly. Peel and
chop the onions up small and fry them gently in the oil until just transparent. Chop up the
kidneys into fairly small pieces, fry very briefly and put in a mixing bowl with the fried
onions. Add the cut up tomatoes, the herbs, the garlic, salt and black pepper. Grease a
fairly large pie dish. Spread a thin layer of mashed potato on the bottom. On top of this
spread a layer of the kidney mixture, then a layer of cheese and once again a thin layer of
potato. Repeat this ending up with a thicker layer of potato. Pat the pie down and then
criss-cross the potato with a fork. Dot with butter and sprinkle on a little grated cheese.
Cook in the centre of the oven at Gas 4 (350°F/180°C) for 1¼ to 1½ hours until really golden
brown.

MAIN COURSE: A MISCELLANY OF MEAT DISHES

Meat Loaf with Pumpkin   page 74
Putney Pancake Parcel   75
Veal Slices with Sage and Parsley   76
Stuffed Cabbage Leaves with Dill Seeds   77
Pork Seed Cakes   77
Marinated Lamb Fillets with Cumin   78
Chicken Breasts with Ladies' Fingers   79
Breasts of Chicken Stuffed with Smoked Fish in a
    Mushroom and Prawn Sauce   80
Chicken Breasts and Almonds in Creamy Cheese
    Sauce   81
Chicken and Nutmeg Lasagne   82
Rabbit with Green Sauce and Pine Nuts   83
Sweetbread Risotto   84
Sautéed Kidneys in Brandy and Orange Sauce   85
Calves' Liver with Gooseberry Sauce   86

COLD DISHES

Cold Spiced Ham Baked in Black Treacle   87
Quick Curried Sauce for Cold Chicken or Turkey   88

Meat Loaf with Pumpkin

1 lb minced beef (450 g)
4–6 tablespoons tomato ketchup
1 breakfastcup porridge oats
thyme
powdered cumin
1 large onion – chopped very finely
2 eggs – whisked
olive oil
butter
salt, black pepper
1½–2 lb pumpkin (700–900g)

This is my version of the American meat loaf which I find very useful for family lunches as it is easy to do, popular and economical. You can try out all sorts of variations of herbs and spices in it, but the main thing with minced meat is that it should be really strongly flavoured, otherwise you can get that terrible grey, tasteless slab. The pumpkin goes very well with the loaf as a vegetable, and you can now get pumpkins in several greengrocers and markets. If you can't find any, substitute marrow. If there is any loaf left over, the meat loaf is good cold.

FOR THE LOAF. In a mixing bowl combine well with a wooden spoon the minced meat, about 1 dessertspoon thyme and the same of powdered cumin, the tomato ketchup, the porridge oats, the finely chopped onion, the whisked eggs, plenty of black pepper and salt. Pack the mixture into a loaf tin or any container which it fills completely, then turn it out again (you will probably need to give it a hard shake) into a greased roasting tin. Brush the loaf all over with tomato ketchup and bake in the middle of the oven at Gas 3 (325°F/160°C) for 1–1½ hours until golden brown.

FOR THE PUMPKIN. Peel, take the seeds out and chop up the pumpkin. Melt about a tablespoon of olive oil and 1–2 oz butter (25–50 g) in a large frying pan. Put the pumpkin in and stir it in the fat. Sprinkle generously with black pepper and salt. Cook very gently, stirring often until the pumpkin is tender – about 20 minutes. Put into a dish and serve with the meat loaf.

Putney Pancake Parcel

FOR THE PANCAKES
4 oz plain wholemeal flour (110 g)
½ teaspoon salt
1 egg
½ pint milk (275 ml)

FOR THE FILLING
1½ lb minced beef (700 g)
2 onions – chopped
handful of fresh basil (if available or
else tarragon or parsley) – chopped
1 dessertspoon oregano
1 teaspoon powdered nutmeg
1 large clove crushed garlic
6 oz mushrooms – sliced (175 g)
2–3 large tomatoes – chopped small
tablespoon tomato purée
1 tablespoon grated Parmesan
salt, black pepper

This is really like a large stuffed savoury pancake – if you have the time you can stuff each pancake separately as they look very impressive all on a dish together. The wholemeal flour makes the pancakes nutty and the strongly favoured mince is a good combination. You can prepare this dish well in advance and keep it warm in the oven.

If you have a blender simply put the flour, salt, egg and half the milk in and whizz up – add the rest of the milk and whizz until smooth. If you have no blender beat ingredients with a wooden spoon until smooth. Heat a little oil in a heavy frying pan until smoking. Pour on about 2–3 tablespoons of batter and spread all over the surface of the pan. When cooked on one side turn over or toss and transfer the cooked pancake to a plate. Continue like this adding more oil when you need to until you have used all the batter and have a pile of pancakes. Keep them warm in a very low oven while you prepare the filling.

Fry the onions gently in a little olive oil until transparent and soft – put on one side. Then gently fry the mushrooms until soft and add to the onions. Then fry the tomatoes and also put them with the onions and mushrooms. Fry the mince in a little fat, digging at it with a wooden spoon to separate it. Stir in the salt, pepper, the crushed garlic, the tomato purée, oregano, chopped fresh herbs and the nutmeg. When the mince is cooked add the onion, mushrooms and tomatoes to it. Now line a shallow serving dish with the pancakes so that they come right over the edges – use a little over half the pancakes for this. Put the mince and vegetable mixture into the serving dish on top of the pancakes. Cover with the rest of the pancakes turning over the edges from underneath, dot with butter, sprinkle with grated Parmesan, cover with foil and keep warm in a low oven until you want to eat it. Just serve with a fresh green vegetable or a salad and perhaps some new potatoes if you are feeling very hungry.

Veal Slices with Sage and Parsley

6 large or 12 small slices of stewing veal
(rubbed with olive oil and the juice of 1
lemon and left for several hours at room
temperature)
2 cloves garlic – crushed
bunch of fresh sage leaves – about 20
leaves
small bunch parsley
¼ lb grated Gruyère cheese or the
cheaper Jarlsberg (110 g)
¼ pint single cream (150 ml)
salt, pepper

You only need use stewing meat for this dish but it tastes delicious. You can use pork if you cannot get veal. The meat is much better if it is left to marinate in olive oil and lemon juice for several hours beforehand. Get the butcher to cut you thin slices of stewing veal or pork instead of chopping it up in chunks.

Rub each piece of meat on both sides with crushed garlic. Chop up the sage and parsley leaves as finely as possible and spread them over each piece of meat together with salt and black pepper. Lay the pieces of meat overlapping each other in a gratinée dish. Cover the dish with foil and cook in a low oven at Gas 2 (300°F/150°C) for about 1½ hours until the meat is tender. Take the meat from the oven and cool slightly. Mix the grated cheese into the cream, with salt and plenty of black pepper. Spread this mixture over the meat and quickly put it under a hot grill until the top goes light golden brown. Serve with new potatoes or rice and a fresh green vegetable or a tomato salad.

Stuffed Cabbage Leaves with Dill Seeds

1½ lb minced pork or beef (700 g)
½ lb tomatoes – chopped up small (225 g)
2 tablespoons tomato purée
1 tablespoon of oregano or marjoram leaves
1 large egg – lightly beaten

juice of ½ small lemon
½ wine glass of sherry or stock
1 fairly large cabbage (not the hard white variety)
dill seeds
salt, black pepper
about 1 oz butter (25 g)

This is a particularly easy and good tasting way of making stuffed cabbage, without rice.

Take the leaves off the cabbage and submerge them in boiling, salted water for 2 minutes. Drain. In a mixing bowl put the meat, tomatoes, tomato purée, oregano, beaten egg, salt and plenty of black pepper. Mix well together with a wooden spoon. Butter a large but not too deep casserole dish. Form the mince mixture into medium sized balls and wrap each one in a cabbage leaf. Arrange them in a casserole dish. Pour over lemon juice and sherry or stock. Sprinkle generously with dill seeds and more salt and black pepper. Dot with butter. Cover and cook in the centre of a pre-heated oven Gas 4 (350°F/180°C) for 1–1¼ hours. Serve with boiled potatoes.

Pork Seed Cakes

1 lb minced pork (450 g)
1 teaspoon caraway seeds
1 teaspoon dill seeds
about 4 tablespoons mashed potato (you can use instant mash if you like as it will be well disguised)
2 eggs – beaten

2 tablespoons tomato purée from tube or tin
2–3 teaspoons salt
2–3 teaspoons black pepper
fresh breadcrumbs to coat the cakes in (whizz up some stale bits of bread in the blender)
fat to fry in

These are really a more interesting kind of rissole. I often do them for lunch as adults and children seem to like them equally. Ask your butcher to mince you some ordinary casserole pork. To serve I think they go best with a salad.

In a mixing bowl put all the ingredients and mix thoroughly with a wooden spoon. It should be a fairly stiff mixture which you can easily form into balls – add more mashed potato if it looks too soft. Form to about the size of ping-pong balls and roll all over in the breadcrumbs. Melt some fat in a heavy frying pan and fry over a medium heat, turning once or twice until the cakes are golden brown all over. If you are not ready to eat them they can be kept warm in a serving dish in a low oven.

Marinated Lamb Fillets with Cumin

6 small lamb neck fillets or 1½–1¾ lb
boneless lamb (700–800 g)
2 medium-sized onions
powdered cumin
Salt, pepper
juice of 1 large lemon
olive oil
¼ pint cream (150 ml)

If the lamb is marinated long enough this can really be a "melt in the mouth" dish. Buy English or Welsh lamb if it is in season because it is so much better that it is worth the slight extra cost.

Put the lemon juice and about 2 tablespoons of olive oil into a roasting dish. Put in the lamb fillets sprinkled on both sides with black pepper and turn about in the mixture. Leave in a cool place, covered with a cloth or foil for about 8 hours, or overnight. Turn the fillets over whenever you remember and spoon some of the mixture over them. When marinated, pour off the surplus mixture, sprinkle the fillets generously with powdered cumin. Fry very gently and slowly in a heavy pan, turning several times, for about 15–25 minutes. Transfer to a serving dish and keep warm. Slice the onions in rings as finely as possible Fry them gently in the leftover fat and juices in the frying pan until transparent but not very soft. Arrange on top of the fillets. Heat the sour cream with any leftover juices in the frying pan just to boiling point. Pour over the fillets and serve. I think this dish is very good with new potatoes and a bean salad.

Chicken Breasts with Ladies' Fingers

6 boned chicken breasts (available at
some branches of Sainsbury's or Marks
& Spencer)
salt, black pepper
1 clove garlic, crushed
1 clove garlic, chopped
½ lb tomatoes, chopped (225 g)
1 large green pimento, chopped
6 oz okra (175 g) — available in markets
and at Indian and Cypriot grocers. The
Indian name for them is Bindhi.
handful of mint leaves — roughly chopped
olive oil
butter

Between the ages of seven and ten I lived in the dusty city of Damascus, in a large, cool house with fountains, palm trees and white fan-tailed pigeons in the garden. When I was not making mud houses in the dust with the gardener's children, or being grilled by my strict Scots governess, I spent my time in the kitchen. I loved nibbling the freshly made flat bread and tasting the sharp-flavoured apricots which dried in the sun on the flat roof outside. I liked seeing the basket of unusual fruit and vegetables which the cook brought in from the market, and I thought that "ladies' fingers", which they called okra, was the most strange and magical vegetable of them all. Now you can buy them fresh in any town or city where there is a Cypriot or Indian community, so here is an easy way to use them.

Rub the chicken breasts with the crushed garlic, salt, pepper and a little olive oil. Fry very gently in a little butter until done, about 20 minutes, turning once or twice. Arrange them on a serving dish and leave in a very low oven to keep warm. In a deep frying pan, preferably with a lid, heat some olive oil and add the chopped tomatoes, pimento, and the okra with the heads and tails cut off, salt, black pepper and the chopped garlic. Stir well together. Cover the pan with a lid or foil and simmer gently for 20–30 minutes, stirring occasionally. Stir in the chopped mint leaves, pour the mixture on top of the chicken breasts and serve with dish of long-grain rice.

Breasts of Chicken Stuffed with Smoked Fish in a Mushroom and Prawn Sauce

6 boned chicken breasts
¾ lb smoked cod fillets (350 g)
3–4 large cloves garlic – crushed
1 level teaspoon fennel seeds
1 tablespoon chopped chives or fennel
leaves
6 oz button mushrooms – sliced thinly
sideways (175 g)
2–3 oz peeled prawns (50–75 g)
a large glass white wine
8 fl oz single cream (225 ml)
½ oz plain flour (10 g)
1 dessertspoon lemon juice
a little chopped parsley as decoration
– optional
a little oil
butter

This strange combination smells and tastes extremely good and the flavour of the sauce is wonderful. It is an exotic looking dish which is simple to make. If you can't get the ready boned chicken breasts an obliging butcher would probably bone some breasts for you.

Butter a fairly large ovenproof gratinée dish. Lay out the chicken breasts flesh side up and rub them with the crushed garlic. Sprinkle them with plenty of black pepper and salt. Chop the fish up into small cubes and put it in a mixing bowl. Stir the chopped chives or fennel leaves and the fennel seed and some more black pepper thoroughly into the fish. Put a spoonful of this mixture in the centre of each chicken breast and fold the breast over the fish. Put these little parcels into the gratinée dish with the folded over ends underneath so that they do not flap open and let all the fish stuffing out. You will find that when they have cooked they will stay together. Brush the tops with a little oil and sprinkle with salt and cook in the centre of the oven at Gas 5 (375°F/190°C) for three quarters of an hour. When they are done pour any juice that has come out of them while cooking into another receptacle. Return the stuffed breasts to a low oven to keep them warm while you make the sauce. Melt about ½ oz butter (10 g) in a heavy-based saucepan and blend into it the plain flour. Let it bubble gently, stirring, for 1–2 minutes. Gradually stir in the juice from the stuffed breasts, the lemon juice and the white wine. Bubble gently, stirring all the time, for 2–3 minutes. Stir in the mushrooms and bubble a minute more. Then stir in the prawns and finally the cream. Check seasoning. Pour this sauce on top of the stuffed breasts and serve. A little chopped parsley sprinkled round the edges looks very pretty. Serve with rice or new potatoes and either a salad or a fresh vegetable.

Chicken Breasts and Almonds in Creamy Cheese Sauce

5–6 chicken breasts
6 oz button mushrooms – sliced
(175 g)
½ oz cornflour (10 g)
1½ oz butter (40 g)
½ pint milk (275 ml)
4 oz grated Cheddar cheese (110 g)
½ pint single cream (275 ml)
2 egg yolks
1 large clove garlic – crushed
sprinkling of grated Parmesan
salt, black pepper
3 oz flaked almonds (75 g)
1 dessertspoon dried oregano

Rub the chicken breasts with a little butter or oil and roast them for 30 minutes in a fairly hot oven, Gas 6 (400°F/200°C). Slice them into thin slices and arrange in a large earthenware dish. Fry the sliced mushrooms gently in two thirds of the butter until only just softened. Fry the flaked almonds in the butter until just golden. Add most of the flaked almonds to the chicken and mushrooms in the earthenware dish but reserve about a quarter of the nuts for final decoration. Sprinkle all with oregano. Keep warm. Make a white sauce by melting the remaining butter in a heavy medium-sized saucepan. Stir in the cornflour until smooth. Fairly gradually add the milk. Bring to the boil and simmer for 3 minutes stirring frequently. Add the grated Cheddar and crushed garlic and stir until melted. Take off the heat and stir the cream and the egg yolks. Put back on a gentle heat, add salt and black pepper to taste and heat up but do not boil. Pour over the chicken, mushrooms and almond mixture. Sprinkle top with grated Parmesan and finally the reserved almonds. Serve, or keep it warm in a low oven until you are ready to eat it. I think this is best eaten with fresh crispy bread and a salad but you could have new potatoes or rice, and broccoli would go very well with the cheesy sauce.

Chicken and Nutmeg Lasagne

about 8 oz (225 g) green lasagne pieces
(lasagne verdi)
cooked meat from 2½ lb chicken (a
generous kg), about 8–10 oz boned
weight (225–275 g) – chopped into
small cubes
6 oz mushrooms – sliced (175 g)
approximately 1¾ pints fairly thick
white sauce (1 litre)
1 tablespoon oil
1 teaspoon grated nutmeg
8 oz grated cheese (225 g)
1 large clove garlic – crushed
1 large egg – lightly whisked
a little grated Parmesan
salt, pepper
butter

A good lasagne is such a useful dish because although it takes a little time to prepare it can be made in advance and only needs a simple salad as an accompanying dish. This creamy chicken and mushroom lasagne tastes really delicious and not at all heavy. The nutmeg somehow brings out the flavours beautifully. This recipe could also be a more unusual addition to that endless list of ways to use up leftover Christmas turkey. You should be able to buy green lasagne in packets in any good grocer or delicatessen – it is now possible to buy lasagne pieces which are ready for the oven and need no boiling first. If you can find this kind it saves a lot of time.

Boil the pieces of lasagne about 4 at a time in plenty of boiling salted water with a tablespoon of oil stirred into it. They take about 10–15 minutes. As each batch is cooked lay the pieces on a clean cloth to drain. Add the grated cheese (not the Parmesan), the crushed garlic, the nutmeg, salt and black pepper to the white sauce and heat until the cheese has completely melted. Take off the heat and stir in thoroughly the lightly whisked egg. Reserve ½ pint (275 ml) or a little more of this sauce for the top. Stir the cooked chopped chicken and sliced mushrooms into the remaining sauce. Butter a large shallow ovenproof dish and arrange a layer of lasagne pieces on the bottom. Cover this with a layer of the chicken, mushroom and sauce mixture, then another layer of lasagne and so on, ending with a layer of lasagne. Spread the remaining cheese sauce on top of this, sprinkle liberally with grated Parmesan and dot with butter. If you have prepared it in advance, put the dish in the fridge until you want to cook it. Bake in the centre of the oven at Gas 4 (350°F/180°C) for about 40 minutes until golden brown on top. Serve it with a tomato and crisp lettuce salad.

Rabbit with Green Sauce and Pine Nuts

FOR THE GREEN SAUCE
The quantities for these are only
approximate — it will not matter if they
are not exact.
juice of 1 small lemon
10–12 tablespoons olive oil
2 large cloves garlic — peeled
2–3 oz fresh basil, parsley and
mint — or whatever you can get (50 –
75 g)
2–4 teaspoons capers
1½ oz grated Parmesan (40 g)
about 2 tablespoons pine
nuts — available in Greek and Cypriot
shops or delicatessens
salt, black pepper

FOR THE RABBIT
1 good joint of rabbit per person
salt, pepper
olive oil

This is my version of an Italian green sauce and is a cross between salsa verde and pesto sauce. I think it is so good on all kinds of pasta and very good indeed poured over large dishes of thinly carved cold veal, pork or lamb at parties. It is best made with quite a lot of fresh basil which is what gives it the very special taste that may bring vividly back the smell and feel of a visit to Italy. But if you have no basil you can make it with parsley, and I add capers and perhaps some mint leaves. Fresh fennel or dill leaves also are very good in this sauce, and lovage in small quantities. The Italians often grind pine nuts up in the sauce but I prefer to sprinkle them on top. You can make the sauce in advance as it is cold and you put it over the food at the last moment. It only takes a moment to make in a liquidiser but if you do not have one you must chop the herbs very finely before mixing them with the other ingredients.

Put all the ingredients except for the nuts into a blender and whizz up for a moment or two until thick and fairly smooth.

Salt and pepper the rabbit joints and spoon a little olive oil over each. Put the joints either into a shallow earthenware dish which you can serve from or into a roasting pan. Cover the dish with foil and cook in the centre of the oven Gas 5 (375°F/190°C) for 1½–2 hours. Then drain the juices from the rabbit (which you should keep as they make a good jellied stock), and if you cooked it in a roasting pan, transfer the joints to a large shallow serving dish. Then spoon the green sauce thickly over each joint and sprinkle with pine nuts. I think this is good served with buttered noodles and carrots, or perhaps a tomato salad.

Sweetbread Risotto

1 lb lambs' sweetbreads (450 g)
1 breakfast cup rice
2½ cups salted water
pinch saffron — or 1 teaspoon turmeric
1 red pepper
1 large onion
½ lb mushrooms (225 g)
1 tablespoon oregano or thyme
salt, black pepper
olive oil

All the books say that you must first soak the sweetbreads in cold salted water for 2–4 hours, drain them and then bring them to the boil with fresh water and a squeeze of lemon. Then you should drain and let them go cold and take off any surplus skin before using. I have cooked them without any preparation at all and they seem to taste just as good, so you can do what you feel like. In any case they make a delicious and less usual risotto, with their mild buttery flavour. Use the short-grain Italian rice they use for risotto if you can get it, otherwise any short-grain rice.

Cook the rice first — bring the salted water to the boil, then stir in the rice and the saffron or turmeric, put a lid on the pan and simmer gently for 10–20 minutes, according to the type of rice used, but be sure to test it to see it does not get over-cooked. It ought still to have a slight nutty bite to it — what is known in Italy as "al dente". Strain the rice into a sieve and run hot water through it. Put it into a covered bowl with a knob or two of butter in a very low oven while you cook the rest of the ingredients. Chop up the pepper and the onion into small pieces. Fry these in a large pan until just tender in a little olive oil and butter. Transfer to the rice dish. Slice the mushrooms thinly across in mushroom shapes, add more olive oil and butter to the pan and fry very gently until the mushrooms are only just soft. Transfer them to the rice dish. Chop up the sweetbreads into very small pieces. (If you like you can be cooking them in another pan while you fry the vegetables.) Melt 1–2 oz butter (25 –50 g) in the pan and gently fry the sweetbreads in it, tossing them about a lot for 3–5 minutes. Transfer them and the butter in the pan to the dish with the other ingredients. Salt and pepper and mix all well together. You can keep this risotto warm in a very low oven for an hour or two if you want to. Serve with a salad.

Sautéed Kidneys in Brandy and Orange Sauce

12 lambs' kidneys (if you use the
smaller New Zealand kind you may
need more)
2 large onions
1 dessertspoon oregano or rosemary
about 3 tablespoons plain flour
seasoned with plenty of black pepper
and a very little salt
juice of ½ lemon
juice of 1 orange
1–2 tablespoons brandy – to taste
¼ pint single cream (150 ml)
2 oz butter (50 g)
olive oil
small bunch parsley chopped – as a
garnish

I often do kidneys like this for our supper after a busy day with no time to cook. They are so quick and easy to do and yet taste delicious. Try to get fresh English lambs' kidneys because they are larger, more tender and better tasting. If your butcher ever has calves' kidneys I think they are even better still.

Skin and slice the kidneys fairly thinly removing the core. Peel and chop up the onions into small pieces or rings. Melt the butter and a little olive oil in a large heavy based pan. Dip the kidney slices into the seasoned flour and put them with the onions in the pan. Fry very gently for about 3–5 minutes. Stir in the herbs and the lemon and orange juice. Simmer very gently for about 10 minutes. Then stir in the brandy and finally just roughly stir in the cream. Transfer to a serving dish. If you need to you can keep this dish warm covered with foil on a low shelf in a very low oven. Before serving sprinkle the chopped parsley over the top. Serve with rice or mashed potatoes and either a fresh green vegetable or a salad.

Calves' Liver with Gooseberry Sauce

about 1¼ lb calves' liver — cut very thinly
(575 g)
seasoned flour
2 onions
3–4 tomatoes
1 wineglass sherry
1 wineglass water
1 small tin gooseberries — drained (in
summer you could use stewed fresh
gooseberries)
handful of fresh mint leaves — roughly
chopped
4 teaspoons capers
salt, black pepper
olive oil
butter

This is a fairly rich tasting and exotic looking dish suitable for a dinner party. If you can't get calves' liver use lambs' — though calves' is much more tender and delicious. If you use lambs' liver try and buy some which is a pale colour. Butchers always say the colour makes no difference but it seems to me that the paler it is the better it tastes. Also ask the butcher to slice the liver as thinly as possible — somehow English butchers never seem to slice it as thinly as in Italy, but you can try to persuade them. Liver is often good mixed with slight sweetness, like orange juice, or as in this recipe where the gooseberries give it an original taste which goes well with the savoury flavour of the mint and capers.

Coat the liver slices in seasoned flour. Melt a little olive oil and about 1 oz butter (25 g) in a large frying pan. Sauté the liver in a pan over a medium heat for 1–2 minutes on each side. Transfer to a fairly large but shallow serving dish, cover with foil and keep warm in a very low oven. Peel and slice the onions into fine rings. Add more oil and butter to the pan and fry the onions over a medium heat until soft and transparent. Transfer to the serving dish and mix with the liver. Cut the tomatoes up into quarters and fry them in the pan until soft. Arrange them on top of the liver and onions. Now into the pan pour the sherry and water, salt and pepper and boil fiercely until the juice has reduced and thickened. Then stir in the capers, the chopped mint leaves and the drained gooseberries and pour the sauce over the dish of liver. If you put the foil on top of the dish again you can keep it warm in a very low oven for an hour or so until you are ready to eat it. I serve it with new or mashed potatoes and a crisp green salad.

Cold Spiced Ham Baked in Black Treacle

**1 piece of rolled, smoked collar.
Whatever size you need, it will shrink a
bit in the cooking but a 4–5 lb piece
(1.75–2.25 kg) should feed at least 15
people. I do not think it is worth
cooking a smaller piece as it will keep
in the fridge for some time.
1 small tin black treacle (about 6–8
tablespoons)
juniper berries
cloves
whole allspice berries
demerara sugar**

*This is a mouthwatering way of cooking smoked, rolled collar or a more expensive joint of
gammon to eat cold. It has a wonderfully mellow, aromatic flavour and you can carve it in
very thin slices. It is perfect for parties or whenever you have to feed a lot of people.*

Soak the piece of bacon in cold water for at least 12 hours, changing the water two or three
times. Then crush some juniper berries in a mortar and poke them right into the bacon with
your fingers where you can, or make incisions if it is rolled so tightly that you can't get your
fingers right in. Stick cloves into the joint all over. Crush the whole allspice in the mortar and
press them as firmly as possible all over the joint too. Spread the black treacle thickly all
over the joint and wrap completely in foil. Bake in a low oven Gas 1 (275°F/140°C) for 4–5
hours according to size. Take out, remove the skin while it is still hot, sprinkle the fat
underneath with demerara sugar and wrap again in foil. Put the joint on a plate with a
board on top and weight it down with weights or books. Leave overnight. Before carving,
unwrap and sprinkle some more demerara sugar on the fat. To store in the fridge cover
again with foil.

Quick Curried Sauce for Cold Chicken or Turkey

**one third mayonnaise (a good, bought
kind will do if you do not have time to
make any)**
two thirds plain yoghurt
lemon juice – to taste
**curry paste (available in jars at Indian
grocers) – added to taste**
Patak's Tikka paste
salt

*Cold chicken or turkey is often dry and sometimes rather tasteless but nevertheless
whether it is after Christmas or after Sunday lunch we often have it left over. This very
quickly made sauce has a good and unusual taste and really makes the cold meat more
interesting. It is also very good for parties as it can be spread all over the meat on a large dish
well in advance and will not go dried up or discoloured. It has a shiny bloom and looks very
appetising decorated with chopped parsley. Patak's Tikka paste is an optional ingredient
but it makes the sauce much better. You should be able to find it in most Indian grocers and
it is very useful to have in your store cupboard for brushing on grills, roasts, or things you
are going to barbecue – in fact whenever you feel you would like an Indian taste to your
meal. Make the quantity of sauce according to the amount of cold chicken or turkey you
want to cover with it.*

Carve the bird as thinly as possible and arrange the slices on a flat dish. Mix the mayonnaise
and yoghurt smoothly together. Stir in the lemon juice, curry paste, Tikka paste and salt to
taste. Pour and spread the sauce all over the meat. Decorate with chopped parsley and
perhaps some nuts or sesame seeds if you have any.

VEGETABLES

Tomatoes and Potatoes with Cream and Garlic   page 90
Really Good Roast Potatoes   90
Root Vegetables with Cream and Watercress   91
Brussels Sprouts with Almonds and Nutmeg Cream   91

SALADS

Primrose Salad   92
Water Melon Salad   92
A Special Tomato Salad   93
Carrot, Hazelnut and Watercress Salad   93
Macaroni in Mayonnaise   94
Quick Bean Salad   94

DRESSINGS

French Dressing   95
Tarragon Dressing for a Lettuce Salad   95

Tomatoes and Potatoes with Cream and Garlic

1 lb potatoes – peeled and boiled in
salted water (450 g)
1–1½ lb tomatoes (450–700 g)
2 cloves garlic – crushed
1 dessertspoon oregano or thyme

½ pint single cream (275 ml)
butter
salt, black pepper
parsley to decorate

Apart from its creamy and delicious flavour this dish is useful as you do not need to serve a second vegetable, and because it is cooked in a casserole dish it can be made in advance and kept warm. It goes best with roast or fried meat or chicken, and is ideal with grilled or baked fish.

Slice the boiled potatoes across into medium-sized slices. Pour boiling water over the tomatoes, and then put them in cold water and peel off the skins. Slice fairly thickly. In a casserole dish put a layer of potatoes, a little crushed garlic, a dot or two of butter, a sprinkling of salt and pepper, a layer of tomatoes, a sprinkling of herbs and so on until the ingredients are used up ending with a layer of tomatoes. Pour the cream over the vegetables. Cover the dish and cook in the centre of a medium oven Gas 4 (350°F/180°C) for about half an hour. Before serving sprinkle some chopped parsley over the top.

Really Good Roast Potatoes

large potatoes   good dripping

It may seem to you unnecessary to have a recipe for roast potatoes but I am always asked how I do them by people who say they produce soggy failures, and although there is no real secret I will write my method down. I learned how to do them from my mother, a good cook in every way, but her golden crisp and crunchy gems earned her the name in our family of "Roast Potato Queen".

Peel the potatoes and cut into small pieces (this is important), about 1–2 in (2.5–5 cm) across. Boil the potatoes in salted water for 15 minutes and drain. Put the oven on Gas 8 (450°F/230°C) and heat up enough dripping to cover up to ½ in (1 cm) or so in a roasting pan. Put in the potatoes and turn them so that they are all covered in melted dripping. Roast towards the top of the oven for ½–¾ hour until they are crisp looking outside and turning golden brown. If you are in a hurry go on cooking on Gas 8 (450°F/230°C) until they are deep rich golden brown – about another half hour – but keep checking as it can vary. However, I think they are even more delicious if after ½–¾ hour on Gas 8 (450°F/230°C) you turn the gas down to Gas 4 (350°F/180°C) until they are really done which usually takes about 1½–2 hours in all. Drain the fat thoroughly off them, put them in a hot serving dish and sprinkle with salt, preferably sea salt.

Root Vegetables with Cream and Watercress

¾–1 lb turnips (350–450 g)
¾–1 lb swede (350–450 g)
1 bunch watercress – chopped up
finely
sprinkling of grated nutmeg
2–3 tablespoons double cream
black pepper

People are often very scathing about swedes and turnips but I think that if they are well cooked and imaginatively used they can be delicious. This is a good combination which goes well with a roast joint. The clear orange, white and green appearance of the vegetables is very appetising.

Peel both the turnip and swede and cut up into chunks. Boil in salted water for 20–30 minutes until tender. Drain and transfer to a serving dish, dot with butter and sprinkle with nutmeg and black pepper. Just before serving sprinkle the chopped watercress amongst the vegetables and stir it in a bit. Spoon the cream over the vegetables.

Brussels Sprouts with Almonds and Nutmeg Cream

1 lb small brussels sprouts (450 g)
¼ pint single cream (150 ml)
1 teaspoon grated nutmeg
2 oz whole blanched almonds (50 g)
butter

Brussels sprouts seem to linger in the shops for so long that it is refreshing to cook them in different ways. A creamy purée is very good and so is this way, which enhances their nutty flavour with nutmeg and the crunchy taste of real nuts.

Put the prepared sprouts in boiling, salted water and simmer for 8–10 minutes until just tender. They should still be bright green and slightly crisp. Drain, put in a warm serving dish and dot with butter. Stir the nutmeg into the cream and pour over the sprouts. Cover with foil and keep warm on top of the oven or in a very low oven. Melt a little butter in a frying pan and toss the almonds in the butter very briefly over a high heat until they go just golden brown. Sprinkle over the sprouts and serve.

Primrose Salad

4 oz small spinach leaves (110 g)
about 10–12 young primrose leaves and
a few flowers (optional)
3–4 oz fresh bean sprouts – if
unavailable substitute 1 red
pepper – sliced finely (75–110 g)
French dressing

Young primrose leaves have a strong, slightly hot flavour. Disraeli's favourite salad is said to have been a combination of primrose shoots and cowslips. Cowslips seem to have almost disappeared from the countryside but primrose leaves mixed with small spinach leaves and crunchy white bean sprouts make an unusual and economical spring salad. You must use fresh bean sprouts as the tinned ones are too soft. Fresh bean sprouts can be bought at some greengrocers and at Chinese grocers. Or you can easily grow your own from the little round Mung beans they sell for the purpose in health food shops. They take two to four days to sprout kept damp in a covered bowl and they will then stay fresh in a polythene bag in the fridge for at least a week.

Very roughly slice the spinach leaves unless they are very small. Mix them in a bowl with the primrose leaves and the bean sprouts. Dress with French dressing. Sprinkle the flowers on the top for a pretty and romantic touch, but they are also good to eat.

Water Melon Salad

1 water melon – or half if a whole one
seems much too large
1 large Spanish onion
juice of ½–1 lemon
olive oil
salt, black pepper
paprika

Using water melon as a savoury salad is unusual and decorative and it goes well with ham or other cold meats.

Peel, thinly slice and remove the pips from the water melon. Slice the onion in very thin rings and mix with the water melon slices in a fairly deep salad bowl. Cover with a plate and leave for half an hour. Mix up a dressing of lemon juice and twice as much olive oil well seasoned with salt and black pepper. Pour this over the melon and onion, sprinkle with paprika and serve.

A Special Tomato Salad

about ½ a small loaf of crumbled stale
bread
1½ lb tomatoes – thinly sliced (700 g)
small handful of fresh basil leaves, or
fresh marjoram leaves or
parsley – chopped
1 large Spanish onion – chopped small
French dressing

Nothing makes a tomato salad more delicious than the flavour of fresh basil, but if you cannot get any you will have to use either fresh marjoram leaves or just parsley. This is a layered salad which should be served very cold.

Put a layer of stale breadcrumbs in a salad bowl, then a layer of finely sliced tomatoes, then a sprinkling of chopped basil and then a thin layer of chopped onion. Repeat these layers until all the ingredients are used up ending with a layer of onion. Pour over a well seasoned French dressing and chill in the fridge before serving.

Carrot, Hazelnut and Watercress Salad

¾ lb carrots (350 g)
2 oz hazelnut kernels (50 g)
1 bunch watercress – roughly chopped
French dressing

If you are really in a hurry you can use tinned carrots for this salad, otherwise you should use fresh baby carrots or the small Dutch ones.

Prepare the carrots and leave them whole if they are very small. Boil them in salted water until not quite tender. Drain. When they are cool put them in a salad bowl and mix the watercress and the hazelnuts in amongst them. Toss with the French dressing.

Macaroni in Mayonnaise

cooked, cold macaroni
enough mayonnaise to really envelop
the macaroni (use home-made
mayonnaise if possible but if you are
in a hurry use a good commercial
mixture like Hellman's Real
Mayonnaise which is quite all right).
black pepper
large bunch of chives — chopped

*You won't think this sounds a good combination, but it is and it is very good for cold meals
and with other salads.*

All you do is mix the mayonnaise, the black pepper and a lot of chopped chives in with the
macaroni. Put the mixture in a serving dish and sprinkle a few more chives on top.

Quick Bean Salad

1 large tin broad beans
1 small red cabbage
1 tin white haricot beans (available
from delicatessens)
oil and vinegar dressing

*Salads made from dried beans soaked overnight and then boiled mixed up with chopped
raw onions are very delicious but they need some forethought. If you are in a rush you
could always keep some tins of beans in your cupboard to make this useful salad. You can
use either raw red cabbage or raw onion.*

Take off the outer leaves of the red cabbage and chop into fine small pieces. Put into a salad
bowl with the drained tinned beans. Toss with a strongly seasoned oil and vinegar dressing.

French Dressing

one third red wine vinegar
a generous two thirds olive oil
1 teaspoon soft brown sugar (for about
7 fl oz/200 ml of dressing)
1 teaspoon mild French
mustard – preferably the whole seed
type
a generous sprinkling of black pepper
and crushed sea salt
a sprinkling of Knorr Aromat Seasoning
to taste

Most people have their own way of making French dressing and adding different things to it. I am always changing mine but one cheating addition which I feel rather ashamed to disclose but which seems to make a great difference, is a sprinkling of Knorr Aromat Savoury Seasoning or another seasoning called Accent.

Mix all the ingredients together thoroughly. I find much the easiest way to mix a dressing is to put the ingredients into a jam jar with a screw-on lid and then shake together vigorously.

Tarragon Dressing for a Lettuce Salad

the yolks of 2 hard-boiled eggs
wine vinegar
1–2 teaspoons mild French mustard
olive oil
salt, black pepper
about 1 tablespoon of tarragon
leaves – chopped finely

Crush the yolks to a paste in a bowl and add a teaspoon of wine vinegar, the mustard, about 1 level teaspoon of salt and a level dessertspoon of black pepper. Beat together thoroughly and then add gradually 6–8 tablespoons of olive oil and 1–2 teaspoons of wine vinegar. Taste to get it as you like it. Finally add the chopped tarragon and pour the dressing over a lettuce salad. If you like, scatter the egg whites, finely chopped, over the lettuce leaves.

PUDDINGS

Tropical Fruit Salad page 99
Summer Fruit on Yoghurt and Whipped Cream
   with Hard Sugar Top 99
Raspberries Wrapped in Creamed Cottage Cheese
   in a Crisp Meringue Case 100
Summer Loaf 101
Fresh Fruit Pudding 101
Apple with Special Meringue 102
Apricot Apples Baked with Rum 103
Crunchy Layered Strawberry Tart 104
Rose Petal Tart 105
Fresh Raspberry and Redcurrant Tart 106
Strawberry or Raspberry Cheesecake 107
Blackcurrant and Almond Chocolate Flan 108
Cashew Nut Fruit Pie 109
Autumn Pie with Almond Crust 110
Easy French Apple Tart 111
Fresh Mincemeat Plate Pie 112
Apricot and Sour Cream Tart with Orange Pastry 113
Cream Cheese Shortbread Flan 114
Cheese Apples 115
Rose and Rosemary Junket 115
Creamy Kirsch Dessert 116
Fresh Orange Jelly with Flower Water Cream 116

Old Fashioned Nursery Delight   117
Cheating Ice Cream with Hot Rum Sauce   117
Brandy Spice Ice Cream with Hot Cranberry Sauce   118
Creamy Rice with Peaches   119
Caramel Mousse   119
Balkan Syllabub   120
Chilled Brandy Soufflé with Hot Chocolate Sauce   121
Blackcurrant Marble Mousse on a Crust   122
Chocolate Mousse Gâteau   123
Chocolate Mousse Wrapped in Cream Cheese
    and Hazelnuts   124

Tropical Fruit Salad

1 large tin lychees
1 tin guavas
1 large tin blackberries or
blackcurrants or black cherries
1 tin passion fruit (if available)
lemon juice
white rum or Kirsch
1–3 tablespoons flower or rose water

This is wonderfully quick to make. It tastes delicious, scented and unusual and it looks lovely. If you can get any of the fruit fresh all the better, but you will need to add sugar. Most large supermarkets sell tinned exotic fruit in their delicatessen section.

Just empty all the tins into a serving bowl and add the juice of ½ to 1 lemon. Add white rum or Kirsch to taste. A little rose or flower water goes very well with the scented taste of the tropical fruit. You can also make this into a tropical jelly by adding 1 oz dissolved gelatine (25 g) to the fruit and juice mixture.

Summer Fruit on Yoghurt and Whipped Cream with Hard Sugar Top

½ pint whipping cream or double cream
(275 ml)
½ pint plain yoghurt (275 ml)
1–1½ lb strawberries or raspberries or
stoned cherries (450–700 g)
3–4 oz castor sugar (75–110 g)

Oh, the thrill of summer fruit! The excitement of the first glossy red cherries after the endless apples and oranges of grey winter! A simple bowl of summer fruit which you have with cream or lemon juice is perfect. This recipe is a pretty and delicious variation.

Whip up the cream. Mix in the yoghurt, sweetened with a little castor sugar. Spread the mixture on a large flat oval or round dish. Arrange the strawberries, raspberries or cherries on top. Boil up about 3 or 4 oz of castor sugar (75–110 g) with a little water until a drop on a plate goes hard quickly as it cools. Do not boil it so much that it goes brown. Pour the boiled sugar in quick strips over the fruit so it looks all shiny. Serve not more than 2 hours later. Usually a little of the hard sugar melts before you serve it but there are still crackly bits which make a very good contrast with the soft fruit and cream.

Raspberries Wrapped in Creamy Cottage Cheese in a Crisp Meringue Case

FOR THE MERINGUE CASE
6–7 oz icing sugar (175–200 g)
3 egg whites
triple strength rose water (available
from chemists)
or rose essence (available from good
grocers)
a drop of oil

FOR THE FILLING
8 oz fresh or frozen raspberries – if
frozen thaw and drain off the juice
(225 g)
12 oz cottage cheese (350 g)
8 fl oz double cream (225 ml)
1–2 oz icing sugar (25–50 g)
a few drops of rose water or essence
castor sugar to sprinkle on top

It is worth getting the rose water or essence to flavour this luscious-looking dish as it gives a deliciously subtle flavour both to the brittle meringue and to the creamy filling. You can use another flavouring essence if you like but I think rose is by far the most special and very useful to have to flavour all kinds of milk or cream puddings and also fruit salads. If you are using fresh summer fruit strawberries are also good in this dish but the frozen ones are too soggy.

Sift the icing sugar on to a sheet of greaseproof paper or foil. Whisk the egg whites in a bowl until frothy. Whisk in the sugar, a little at a time and add a few drops of rose water or essence to taste. Put the bowl over a saucepan half filled with simmering water and whisk the meringue until it stands in peaks when the whisk is lifted out. Lightly oil a shallow ovenproof flan dish or plate about 8–10 in (20–25.5 cm) in diameter. Spread the meringue smoothly over the bottom of the dish and build it up round the edges in rough flicks. It should come up well over the rim of the dish making a sort of flan case. Put the dish on the bottom shelf of the oven at Gas 1 (275°F/140°C) for 2–2½ hours until the meringue is quite firm. Cool the meringue and leave in a dry place until you are ready to fill it.

Whisk the cream until stiff. Stir in the cottage cheese, the icing sugar and the rose water to taste and half the raspberries. If you are making the pudding well in advance keep the filling in the fridge and fill the case with it nearer the time that you will be eating it. Arrange the other raspberries on top of the filling and sprinkle them with castor sugar. Put the filled case in a cool place or in the fridge until you serve it.

Summer Loaf

1 large white tin loaf – unsliced and
slightly stale
½ lb soft fresh fruit (raspberries,
strawberries, redcurrants, etc) (225 g)

2–3 tablespoons redcurrant jelly
10 oz cream cheese (275 g)
2 tablespoons castor sugar

*This is rather like summer pudding in loaf shape with a sweetened cream-cheese coating.
You can make it with one or more fruits. It is decorative and very delicious.*

With a sharp knife cut loaf lengthwise in thin slices. Cut off the crusts. Put the fruit (any large
strawberries cut in half) into a bowl and bind together with the redcurrant jelly. If the
mixture seems very stiff add a little lemon juice. Layer the fruit mixture and bread in a 2-lb
(1-kg) loaf tin starting and ending with a layer of bread. Put a piece of foil or greaseproof
paper and a book on top of this layered loaf to weight it and leave in a cool place for an hour
or so. Run a knife round the edges and then turn it out on to a serving plate and spread the
cream cheese mixed thoroughly with the castor sugar all over the loaf. Smooth with a
palette knife dipped in cold water. Decorate with a few reserved fruits and perhaps one or
two little strawberry leaves if you have them. Cool in fridge for at least an hour. To eat, cut
in slices downwards and serve with cream.

Fresh Fruit Pudding (serves 8–12)

Victoria sandwich cake mixture using
3 eggs
1–2 lb fresh uncooked fruit (450–900 g)

castor sugar
redcurrant jelly

*This pudding can be made with almost any fresh fruit of the moment, rhubarb, apple,
gooseberries and all the summer fruits, apricots etc. Sharp fruits like rhubarb or blackcurrant are particularly good. It can feed a large number of people and can be made the
day before so it is very good for busy Sunday lunches etc.*

Heat oven to Gas 4–5 (350°F/180°C–375°F/190°C). Make a Victoria sandwich mixture
(you can use wholemeal self-raising flour if you like which gives a nice nutty taste to the
fruit). Put it into a greased flan-quiche dish. A medium sized china one with ripply edges is
best for this. Completely cover the uncooked cake mixture with raw fruit (chopped up
small if it is rhubarb, apples, apricots etc.), and sprinkle castor sugar over the top. Put it in
the middle of the oven for ½ to 1 hour or until the cake has risen and enveloped all the fruit
and is springy to touch and golden brown (it may take longer than an hour). Melt enough
redcurrant jelly in a pan to spread over the top while the pudding is still warm. Cool and
serve in slices with cream.

Apple with Special Meringue

about 6 cooking apples
1 teaspoon powdered mace (optional)
or cinnamon
3 oz dark brown sugar (75 g)
lemon juice from the grated lemon
a little water
6 oz castor sugar (175 g)
3 egg whites (large eggs)
grated rind of 1 large lemon
3 oz chopped nuts or almond flakes
(75 g)

It is always useful to have different apple recipes because there is so much of the year when there is really no other fresh fruit. This simple recipe makes stewed apple or purée more exciting. You could also use it on rhubarb. Remember to grate the lemon rind before you squeeze the juice out.

Stew the apples with the brown sugar and the mace, the lemon juice and a little water. Put in an ovenproof serving dish and let cool. Pre-heat the oven to Gas 6 (400°F/200°C). Whisk the egg whites until stiff. Add the castor sugar (reserve a little for sprinkling on the top) and whisk again. Fold in the lemon rind and nuts. Spoon on top of the apple, sprinkle with castor sugar and bake in the top half of the oven for 10–15 minutes until the meringue is golden brown. If you do not want to serve it at once you can turn down the oven to low for up to an hour or so. Serve with cream.

Apricot Apples Baked with Rum

1 large apple per person
¼–½ lb dried apricots – chopped fairly
small (110–225 g)
1 wineglass dark rum
juice of 1 orange
dark brown sugar
about 3–4 teaspoons powdered
cardamom or mixed spice

I have always loved both baked potatoes and baked apples, and every September we come back from our Arthur Ransome-like summer holidays in Devon laden with huge green apples from the orchard where we stay. For several weeks I try to think up ever-changing apple recipes so that they will get used up. It is not too difficult as apples are versatile and go so well with other fruits and flavourings; with crumbly rich pastry as a traditional apple pie, with flaky pastry in French apple tarts, highly spiced in an old English way, for creamy apple purée, moist apple cake, or just used up in a satisfying way with lemon juice to make pots of apple jelly. Here is a way of baking apples which I think makes them equally suitable for a family meal or a dinner party.

Make a shallow cut round the middle of each apple and core them. Put them in a shallow ovenproof dish, sprinkle with the cardamom or spice. Fill each one with chopped, dried apricots and press down firmly. Pour over the orange juice and rum. Sprinkle over plenty of brown sugar and top each apple with a knob of butter. Bake in the middle of the oven Gas 5 (375°F/190°C) for about 1–1¼ hours. Then drain the juice off into a saucepan, boil it fiercely until it thickens and pour it over the apples just before serving. It makes them look extra shiny and appetising. Serve with cream.

Crunchy Layered Strawberry Tart

FOR THE BASE
6 oz soft brown sugar (175 g)
6 oz butter (175 g)
8 oz quick porridge oats (225 g)

FOR THE MIDDLE
¼ pint soured cream (150 ml)
½ pint plain yoghurt (275 ml)
2 oz castor sugar (50 g)
grated rind of 1 lemon (optional)

FOR THE TOP
¾–1 lb fresh strawberries (or raspberries) (350–450 g)
½ lb redcurrant jelly (225 g)

This is a lovely tart with a flapjack base, a creamy and subtle middle layer and a fruit top. It is simple and quick to make but tastes elaborate. It is best to make with fresh summer fruit on top but in winter you can use some good jam (warmed slightly to make it easy to spread) like black cherry or that delicious Hungarian apricot jam they sell in most supermarkets quite cheaply.

Pre-heat oven to Gas 4 (350°F/180°C). Put the brown sugar and butter into a saucepan and gently melt but do not let it boil. Remove from heat and stir in the porridge oats. Grease a china or aluminium flan dish, about 9–10 in diameter (23–25.5 cm). Put the mixture into the dish and spread evenly. Bake it in the top half of the oven for 15–20 minutes. Cool slightly. Stir the yoghurt, sour cream, sugar and lemon peel together and pour on top of the flapjack base. Put dish back in the oven for 8 minutes. Cool. Slice the strawberries in half and arrange them on top of the soured cream and yoghurt which will have gone smooth and slightly firm. Melt the redcurrant jelly gently and glaze the strawberries with it (I find it easiest using a pastry brush but you can spoon it over if you like). Once you have glazed it keep it in a cool place but not the fridge. You can make the first two layers the day before but do not put the fruit on top sooner than 2 to 3 hours before eating it. Serve with cream, and use a sharp knife to cut into the crisp flapjack base.

Rose Petal Tart

**FOR THE CRYSTALLISED ROSE
PETALS**
petals of 1–2 red roses
1 large egg white – reserve the yolk for
the tart filling
castor sugar

FOR THE PASTRY CASE
8 oz packet puff pastry (225 g)

FOR THE FILLING
½ pint double cream (275 ml)
¼ pint plain yoghurt (150 ml)
1 egg yolk
2 tablespoons castor sugar
2–3 tablespoons rose water or a few
drops of rose essence – to taste

You may feel this sounds too romantic to taste really good. If you have not yet discovered the subtle flavour of rose petals you have a treat in store. They have a definite flavour which is not too scented (some scented flavours can taste too much like cosmetics). I first tried delicious, delicate rose petal jam in Istanbul and my luggage on the return flight was overweight because I could not resist cramming in amongst my holiday clothes several pretty pots of jam with an old-fashioned picture of a crimson rose on the label. Since then I have realised it is easy to make one's own jam out of all those overblown roses which need snipping off throughout the summer. Then there are crystallised rose petals; pretty, unusual and subtly flavoured for decoration of cakes and puddings. The rose water you need for this tart can be bought at Greek, Cypriot and Turkish shops and also at chemists, and is a nice addition to fruit salads. You can make the crystallised petals in advance and keep them in an airtight container until you need them. I think they are a delicious topping for this tart and everyone is always amazed by them. The filling is rather like a very light, rose flavoured cheese cake.

Beat the egg white until stiff. Put some castor sugar in a bowl. Dip each petal in the egg white and then into the castor sugar, and lay on a non-greased baking sheet, or ideally on a piece of non-stick baking paper. Put in the lowest possible oven for about 1–1½ hours until quite dry and crisp. Ease each petal off very carefully with a very thin knife, like a palette knife – some petals always crumble as they are so thin and brittle. Keep in an airtight tin ready to use.

Roll out the pastry to about ⅛ in (3 mm) thick in a roughly circular shape. Grease a shallow 8–9 in (20–23 cm) flan dish. Line the flan dish with the pastry and neaten the edges by folding them over double. Cover the pastry with greaseproof paper or foil weighted down by dried beans or rice and bake blind in a pre-heated oven Gas 6 (400°F/200°C) for 15 minutes. Take the foil and dried beans off and let cool.

In a mixing bowl whisk up double cream until it is thick. Add egg yolk, castor sugar, and the yoghurt and whisk thoroughly together. Gradually add the rose water or rose essence, and whisk in. Pour the mixture into the pastry case and bake in the centre of a pre-heated oven Gas 3 (325°F/160°C) for 20 minutes. Cool in the fridge. Take out of the fridge an hour or so before you eat it. Sprinkle the crystallised rose petals all over the top at the last moment.

Fresh Raspberry and Redcurrant Tart

FOR THE PASTRY
8 oz plain flour (225 g)
1 tablespoon icing sugar
4 oz butter or margarine (110 g)
2 oz lard (50 g)
1 egg yolk and a little cold water to bind
pinch of salt
FOR THE FILLING
¾ lb fresh raspberries (350 g)
½ lb fresh redcurrants (225 g)
redcurrant jelly to glaze

During the summer I am always making these glossy, succulent tarts with fresh summer fruit. They are quick and easy to make and always look beautiful. Every crumb is eaten up with great enthusiasm.

Make the pastry by rubbing together the flour, icing sugar, salt and the fat with your fingertips until it is like breadcrumbs. Mix in the egg yolk and a little cold water with a knife until the mixture just sticks together. Gather into a ball and cool in the fridge for half an hour or more. Heat the oven to Gas 6 (400°F/200°C). Butter a shallow 9 in (23 cm) flan dish. Roll out pastry and line the flan dish with it. Put a piece of greaseproof paper or foil on top filled with dried beans or rice and bake "blind" for about 20 minutes. Take out, lift off the foil and the beans. When cool arrange the raspberries and redcurrants in the flan case. Gently melt about ½ lb redcurrant jelly (225 g) in a saucepan and spoon over the raspberries so that they are all glazed. Cool and eat the same day if possible.

VARIATIONS. Fill with firm dry strawberries cut in half and arranged neatly. Glaze with redcurrant jelly.
Fill with stoned fresh cherries and glaze with redcurrant jelly.
Fill with thinly sliced, neatly arranged fresh peaches and glaze with apple or crab apple jelly. A few fresh redcurrants, if available, among the peach slices add a very complementary sharp flavour and look lovely.
When little green seedless grapes are in season they make a very pretty and fresh tasting filling to a tart. Lime marmalade for the glazing gives a good combination of taste and is the right colour.

Strawberry or Raspberry Cheesecake

6 oz digestive biscuits – crumbled
(175 g)
2–3 tablespoons melted butter
1 heaped tablespoon soft dark brown
(or demerara) sugar
8 oz full cream cheese (225 g)
1 egg – lightly whisked
½ teaspoon vanilla essence
2–3 tablespoons castor sugar
juice of ½ lemon
¾ lb fresh strawberries or raspberries
(350 g)
redcurrant jelly

Of course this lovely pudding is not my invented recipe – it was given to me by an American girl when I was very young and had not even begun to cook yet, but I was already rather greedy and it was one of my first experiments in cooking. The American girl did it without the fruit on top but I think it makes it more delicious and much more exciting looking with the shiny fresh fruit.

Crumble digestive biscuits either in a liquidiser or by hand and mix with about a heaped tablespoon of brown sugar and the melted butter. Put the mixture into an 8 or 9 in (20–23 cm) shallow flan dish. Pat down firmly and smoothly with a metal spoon. Put in the oven Gas 5 (375°F/190°C) for 5 minutes. In a bowl mix up the cream cheese, the egg, ½ teaspoon of vanilla essence, 2–3 tablespoons castor sugar and the juice of ½ lemon. Beat with a wooden spoon or electric whisk. Pour into the biscuit crust and put it into the oven Gas 5 (375°F/190°C) for about 20 minutes until it looks firm. Let it cool. For the fruit top arrange the fruit (for strawberries cut them in half) on top of the cheesecake, then melt about four tablespoons of redcurrant jelly in a saucepan and spoon it out all over the fruit. Again let cool.

Blackcurrant and Almond Chocolate Flan

6 oz chocolate cake mixture (175 g)
(see page 127)
1½ oz flaked almonds (40 g)
½–¾ lb fresh uncooked blackcurrants,
sprinkled with castor sugar (225–350 g)
¼–½ lb redcurrant jelly (110–225 g)

This is a flan which you can make in summer with fresh blackcurrants using the easy chocolate cake recipe – it is easy to make and the sharp taste of the blackcurrants is wonderful combined with the chocolate. It is a luxurious and mouthwatering looking pudding.

Make up the cake mixture and spread into a buttered 9–10 in (23–25.5 cm) flan dish (the china fluted ones are good for this). On top of the cake mixture arrange half the almonds, then the blackcurrants (sprinkled with castor sugar) and finally the other half of the almonds. Put in the centre of the oven Gas 3 (325°F/160°C) and bake for about 1¼–1½ hours until firm to touch in the middle. Melt the redcurrant jelly in a pan and use it to glaze the top of the flan – a pastry brush is useful to spread it all over as you pour it on. Cool and serve with cream.

VARIATION. You can make another version of this lovely pudding by baking the cake mixture in a ring mould tin. When you turn it out melt some redcurrant jelly and (using a pastry brush) brush the cake all over with it to glaze. When cool, fill the middle with fresh whipped cream and, if it's summer, with soft fruit. In winter you can use stewed, drained, dried apricots, drained tinned cherries, or frozen raspberries.

Cashew Nut Fruit Pie

FOR THE PASTRY
12 oz plain flour (350 g)
½ teaspoon salt
6 oz butter or block margarine (175 g)
3 oz lard (75 g)
a little very cold water

FOR THE FILLING
4–5 cooking apples
1 dessertspoon powdered cinnamon
3 tablespoons soft brown sugar
juice of 1 lemon
about 8 oz blackcurrants or
blackberries – fresh or frozen (225 g)
about 6–8 oz gooseberries – fresh,
frozen or tinned ones drained (175–225 g)
4 oz plain cashew nuts – fried briefly in
a little butter until golden brown (110 g)
castor sugar

This is a really delicious fruit pie which has a good mixture of tastes and textures inside and a rich, crumbly pastry on top. If you feel you can't make good pastry do try this kind; perhaps because of the extra fat it never seems to fail and turns out quite melting and delicious. The important thing is not to add too much water. You can buy plain cashew nuts in good grocers or health food stores. Stewed dried apricots are also a wonderful addition to the pie.

Sift the flour and salt into a bowl. Cut the fat into the flour and then rub in lightly with the fingertips until it looks like breadcrumbs. With a round-bladed knife mix in a little very cold water – preferably iced from the fridge – until the mixture only just begins to stick together. Gather up into a ball, wrap in foil or polythene and leave in the fridge for at least an hour or until the next day.

Peel and core the apples and cut up roughly. Stew gently with the brown sugar and very little water until they have gone mushy. Stir in the lemon juice. Put the mixture into a china flan dish or a large sandwich cake tin about 10 in (25.5 cm) in diameter. Allow to cool. Then put the gooseberries on top, then the cashew nuts and finally the blackcurrants or blackberries. Sprinkle castor sugar all over. Roll out the pastry fairly thickly to roughly the size of the flan dish. Roll it back again over the rolling pin and then out again on to the flan dish on top of the fruit. Trim and press down the edges. Roll out the trimmings and decorate with leaves etc. Sprinkle with castor sugar. Bake in the centre of a pre-heated oven Gas 6 (400°F/200°C) for 25–30 minutes until light golden brown. Serve with cream of course.

Autumn Pie with Almond Crust

about 4 large cooking apples
½ lb blackberries (225 g) (optional)
2–3 oz sultanas (50–75 g)
2 teaspoons powdered cardamom
2 teaspoons powdered cinnamon } or 4 teaspoons mixed spice
2 oz soft brown sugar (50 g)

FOR THE PASTRY
4 oz ground almonds (110 g)
4 oz plain flour (110 g)
2 oz lard (50 g)
4 oz butter (110 g)
pinch salt
grated peel of 1 lemon
juice of ½–1 lemon

The point of this recipe is the pastry which is made with ground almonds. It is rich and lemon flavoured and really melts in your mouth. You need not put the spice on the filling if you do not want to, but it makes the apples taste less usual.

Peel the apples and cut into very small pieces, lay them on a large metal or earthenware plate or a shallow flan dish with the sultanas and blackberries. Sprinkle all over with brown sugar and the spices.

Stir the ground almonds and flour, salt and lemon peel together in a mixing bowl. Cut the lard and butter into this mixture and then rub it in with your fingers. Add the lemon juice until the mixture begins to stick together. Gather up in a ball and knead with floured hands on a floured board (pressing it out with the palm of your hand and gathering it up into a ball again) until it is soft, light and pliable. If possible, leave in the fridge for at least an hour before use. Before rolling it out re-knead once or twice, then roll out in a rough circle just a bit bigger than the plate the fruit is on. To cover the apples with it you roll the pastry carefully back over the rolling pin and then out again on to the apples – in this way the pastry will not break up before it reaches the apples. Press the pastry to the side of the dish then trim the edges. Sprinkle with castor sugar and bake in the centre of a pre-heated oven Gas 5 (375°F/190°C) for three quarters of an hour. Serve warm or cold with cream. The pastry is very crumbly indeed so it is easiest to serve it out with a slice or a very wide flat knife.

Easy French Apple Tart

8 oz packet puff pastry (225 g)
5–6 cooking apples
about ¾ jar good apricot jam

Very like those delicious shiny apple tarts which make your mouth water in pâtisseries all over France – but this is really simple to make.

Roll out the pastry very thinly. Lay it on a large flat, buttered baking tin. Fold over the edges by about one inch. Peel the apples and slice very thinly. Arrange the apples neatly overlapping on the pastry leaving the folded edges uncovered. Pre-heat oven to Gas 6 (400°F/200°C) and bake towards the top of the oven for 20–30 minutes or until the pastry round the edge is risen and golden brown. Melt the apricot jam gently in a small saucepan and spoon evenly over the apples spreading it thinly over the pastry edges too. Cool and cut into rectangular slices.

Fresh Mincemeat Plate Pie

FOR THE PASTRY
10 oz plain flour (275 g)
4 oz block margarine or butter (110 g)
3 oz lard (75 g)
pinch salt
a little very cold water

FOR THE FILLING
6 cooking apples
juice of 1 lemon
1—4 tablespoons granulated sugar
3 teaspoons cinnamon
4 oz sultanas (110 g)
2 oz chopped mixed peel (50 g)
2 oranges — peeled, sliced and cut into small pieces
2 oz whole or halved blanched almonds (50 g)
a little butter
a little castor sugar

The filling for this pie gives a taste of Christmas and yet it has a much fresher, sharper taste than real mincemeat. It is a lovely combination of consistencies.

Cut the fat into the flour and salt in a mixing bowl. Rub together with your fingertips until it is like breadcrumbs. Mix in a little very cold water until the mixture just sticks together. Gather into a ball and leave in the fridge for at least 1 hour.

Peel and core the apples and cut into pieces. Put them with the sugar, lemon juice and a very little water in a saucepan. Cover, and simmer gently until the apples are soft. Take them out with a slotted spoon and put them on a large ovenproof plate or a shallow flan dish. Boil up rapidly any liquid left over from the apples until it thickens and pour it over the apples. Sprinkle with the cinnamon, the sultanas, the cut up orange slices and the mixed peel. Fry the almonds quickly in a little butter until just golden and sprinkle them on top of the fruit. Pre-heat the oven to Gas 6 (400°F/200°C). Roll out the pastry to roughly the size of the pie plate. Moisten the edges of the pie plate. Roll the pastry back over the rolling pin and out again on to the fruit. Trim the edges and press down. Decorate with the trimmings cut into shapes (my daughter was given a toy pastry set which has little plastic pastry cutters in the shapes of hearts, stars, birds etc., which are very useful to me — a plump crumbly pie covered with hearts and glistening with castor sugar is a cheering sight). Sprinkle castor sugar over the top and cook in the centre of the oven at Gas 6 (400°F/200°C) for 20–30 minutes until pale golden brown. Serve with cream, hot if possible but it is also good cold.

Apricot and Sour Cream Tart with Orange Pastry

FOR THE PASTRY
8 oz plain flour (225 g)
2 tablespoons icing sugar
4 oz butter or margarine (110 g)
2 oz lard (50 g)
grated rind of one orange
orange juice

FOR THE FILLING
½ pint soured cream (275 ml)
¾ lb dried, stewed apricots (350 g)
4 oz sugar (110 g)

There is something very special about the strong taste of dried apricots. In the winter when fruit is so limited they are invaluable for all sorts of puddings. This is a delicious layered tart. You must prepare the dried apricots in advance. Soak ¾ lb (350 g) in cold water for at least an hour. Then stew in a covered dish in a moderate oven Gas 5 (375°F/190°C) with 4 oz sugar (110 g) and water to cover for about 1½ hours. Cool.

Butter a shallow 9 in (23 cm) flan dish. To make the pastry sift the flour and icing sugar into a mixing bowl, cut in the fat and rub in with your fingertips until it resembles breadcrumbs. Stir in the grated orange rind. Squeeze out the orange juice and slowly stir into the pastry with a knife until the mixture just begins to stick together. Gather into a ball and refrigerate for half an hour or more. Heat oven to Gas 6 (400°F/200°C). Roll pastry out and line flan dish. Put a piece of foil on top filled with dry beans or rice and bake ''blind'' for 20–25 minutes. Take out and pour the soured cream into the pastry case. Put back in the oven for 10 minutes. Cool. Drain the stewed apricots and put the juice in a saucepan. Arrange the apricots on top of the soured cream. Add sugar to the juice and boil up rapidly until it thickens. Cool slightly and spoon over the apricots. Cool and serve.

Cream Cheese Shortbread Flan

FOR THE SHORTBREAD CASE
9 oz plain flour (250 g)
3 oz castor sugar (75 g)
8 oz butter (200 g)

FOR THE FILLING
8 oz cream cheese (225 g)
¼ pint double cream – whipped (150 ml)
2 oz castor sugar – to taste (50 g)
3 oz whole almonds (75 g)
handful of raisins
a little butter
demerara sugar

This simple mixture of cream cheese, whipped cream and sugar is really luxurious tasting. I also use it as a filling for cakes but used in a rich shortbread flan it is specially good.

Grease and flour an 8–9 in (20–23 cm) flan dish. Sift the flour and add the sugar. Knead the butter, keeping it in one piece, into the flour and sugar until they are gradually worked in. Knead well and then press into the flan dish to line it. Prick well and bake until firm and golden at Gas 3 (325°F/160°C) for about three quarters of an hour. Let cool.

In a bowl mix the cream cheese thoroughly with the sugar. Add the whipped cream. Put the mixture into the shortbread crust and smooth top. Toss the almonds in a frying pan in a little butter until just golden brown. Mix with the raisins and put on top of the cream cheese mixture. Sprinkle with demerara sugar and cool in the fridge before serving. Cut up with a sharp knife.

Cheese Apples

¾ lb cream cheese (350 g)
2 oz castor sugar (50 g)
paprika
whole cloves
angelica strips
5–8 fl oz double cream (150–225 ml)

I think that the combination of cream cheese and cream is very good and here the cheese is formed into little mock crab apples which makes a pretty pudding.

Mix the cream cheese thoroughly with the castor sugar. Form the mixture into balls about the size of crab apples. Sprinkle them with paprika and stick one clove into each ball. Soften the angelica strips in hot water and cut out of them enough small leaf shapes to give each cheese apple one or two leaves stuck in the opposite end to the clove. Arrange the apples carefully on a pretty dish and chill in the fridge. Serve with cream.

Rose and Rosemary Junket

1½ pints milk (850 ml)
1 tablespoon castor sugar
4 teaspoons rennet — available from
good grocers, Stones almond-flavoured
is particularly good
¼ pint double cream (150 ml)
3–4 sprigs fresh rosemary
rose flower water (or a few drops of rose
essence)

Junket is even more instant to make than one of the modern instant puddings and with its very special consistency, I think it is an old-fashioned dessert which should be revived. The usual way to serve it is with nutmeg sprinkled on top and a bowl of stewed fruit with it. Here is another way to do it, flavoured delicately with rose and rosemary.

Stir the sugar into the milk in a saucepan, add the sprigs of rosemary and heat the milk but do not boil. Then leave it to cool to blood heat. Remove the rosemary sprigs, add the rennet, put into individual dishes and leave at room temperature to set. Then cool in the fridge. Before serving stir 3–4 teaspoons rose water or a few drops of rose essence into the cream and pour gently on top of the junket.

VARIATION. You can also make honey-flavoured junket by dissolving honey in the milk to sweeten it, then pour cream on the top and sprinkle it with chopped nuts.

Creamy Kirsch Dessert

1½ oz ground rice (40 g)
1 pint milk (570 ml)
grated rind of a lemon
1½ oz granulated sugar (40 g)

1 full sherry glass of Kirsch (or white rum)
¼ pint double cream (150 ml)
rose flower water to taste (optional)
raspberries for the top (fresh or frozen)

This is basically a creamy ground rice pudding flavoured with Kirsch with raspberries on the top which you serve cold. It is very pretty-looking if you put it into individual glass dishes.

Blend the ground rice with a little of the milk. Add the lemon rind and sugar to the rest of the milk and bring to the boil. Add the blended rice, simmer gently, stirring often, for 10–15 minutes. Stir in the Kirsch (and rose water). Taste for flavour and add more Kirsch if you like a strong alcoholic flavour! Let cool. Whip up the cream until thick and then fold into the rice mixture. If the rice seems too thick stir in a little milk first. Spoon into individual dishes. Arrange the raspberries on top, if they are fresh sprinkle castor sugar over them. Serve very cold.

Fresh Orange Jelly with Flower Water Cream

grated rind of 3–4 oranges
juice of 6–9 oranges and of 1
lemon – depending on their size; they
should make about 1¼ pints juice
(720 ml)
2–3 tablespoons orange flower
water – available from chemists and
very useful for adding to fruit salads,
sponge cakes and milk puddings
¾ pint water (425 ml)

4 oz sugar (110 g)
1½ oz gelatine – 2 oz in hot weather
(40–50 g)

FOR THE TOPPING
3 oz chopped nuts (75 g)
½ pint double cream (275 ml)
1½ oz castor sugar (40 g)
1 tablespoon orange flower water

I always think fresh fruit jellies are really refreshing and delicious and they are not much trouble to make. With a layer of crunchy nuts and some rather Middle Eastern tasting orange flower cream on top, this dessert looks very pretty in glass bowls, individual ones if possible but otherwise one large bowl.

Put the grated rind of 3–4 oranges on one side. Squeeze the juice from the oranges and lemon making about 1¼ pints juice (720 ml). Stir in 2–3 tablespoons orange flower water, to taste. Dissolve the sugar and gelatine completely in the water over a medium heat. Mix with the fruit juice and pour into individual dishes. Allow to set. Sprinkle the chopped nuts all over the top of each jelly. Whisk the cream until stiff. Whisk in 1½ oz castor sugar (40 g) and 1 tablespoon orange flower water. Spoon the cream on top of the nuts and decorate with the grated orange rind. Chill in the fridge before serving.

Old Fashioned Nursery Delight

1½ oz tapioca (40 g)
1 pint milk (570 ml)
1 oz sugar (25 g)
grated rind of a lemon
3 egg whites for the meringue top
3 oz chopped nuts (75 g)

2 oz castor sugar (75 g)
3 oz granulated sugar (75 g)
at least 2 or 3 pints (1.15–1.75 litres)
apple or rhubarb purée, or stewed fruit
in a little thick syrup, not swimming in
thin juice. Stewed dried apricots are
very good

Many people are put off by the idea of tapioca, "frog spawn" they say, thinking back to their school days. But professed tapioca haters are converted by eating this luxurious nursery pudding. I am sure there are a lot of people like me who can't resist good nursery food. You can vary this pudding according to the fruit available at the time of the year and also have it hot or cold to go with the weather.

Put the fruit or fruit purée into a deep ovenproof dish, a large Pyrex bowl is good as you see the layers through it. Put the tapioca into a saucepan, add the milk, sugar and the grated peel of a lemon. Bring to the boil stirring, and then simmer, stirring quite often for 30 minutes. Put the tapioca on top of the fruit. Let cool. Whisk the egg whites until stiff. Add the granulated sugar and whisk in well. Fold in the castor sugar and chopped nuts with a metal spoon. Arrange on top of the tapioca. Bake in the top of a fairly hot oven Gas 6 (400°F/200°C) until golden brown, about 8–10 minutes. Serve hot or cold with cream. You can do the fruit and tapioca in advance but the meringue should not be done more than a few hours before eating.

Cheating Ice Cream with Hot Rum Sauce

one packet Bird's Dream Topping
½ pint whipping cream (275 ml)
½ teaspoon vanilla essence
1 tablespoon soft brown or castor sugar
one egg yolk

FOR THE HOT RUM SAUCE
2–3 tablespoons black treacle
2 oz butter (50 g)
3 oz plain chocolate (75 g)
about 2 dessertspoons dark rum
juice of 1 orange

This recipe is easy to make and tastes much more elaborate than it is.

Make up the Dream Topping according to directions. Add vanilla essence and whisk in the sugar and egg yolk. Whisk up the whipping cream and fold into the mixture. Put in a container in the freezing compartment of the fridge for at least three hours, or in the freezer for 1–2 hours.

Put all ingredients in a saucepan. Gently heat and stir, until the chocolate has melted and serve with the ice cream.

Brandy Spice Ice Cream with Hot Cranberry Sauce

2 packets Bird's Dream Topping
¼ pint double cream (150 ml)
1 oz castor sugar (25 g)
1 heaped teaspoon ground mace – this
should be available at good grocers,
Fox's Herbs do it. If you cannot get it,
substitute nutmeg.
1 teaspoon cinnamon
1–2 tablespoons brandy to taste

FOR THE CRANBERRY SAUCE
¾ lb fresh cranberries (350 g)
6 oz granulated sugar (175 g)
½ pint water (275 ml)
about 1 tablespoon lemon juice

Although you may disapprove of making an ice cream so easily and quickly with Bird's Dream Topping I am sure you will agree that it does taste creamy and delicious. It's very quick and doesn't have to be re-whisked halfway through the freezing. The sharp taste and brilliant scarlet appearance of the hot cranberries is lovely.

Make up the Dream Topping according to the directions. Whisk up the cream until thick and then whisk it thoroughly into the Dream Topping mixture with the spices, the sugar and the brandy. Put the mixture in a bowl, sprinkle a little ground mace on top and put it in the freezing compartment of the fridge for at least 3 hours.

Dissolve the sugar in the water in a saucepan and boil for 5 minutes. Add the cranberries, do not cover the pan, and boil for about 5 more minutes. Stir in the lemon juice and pass the sauce round hot with the ice cream.

Creamy Rice with Peaches

1 cup pudding rice
2½ cups water
¼ pint double cream (150 ml)
¼ pint yoghurt (150 ml)
2–3 tablespoons castor sugar – to taste
1 teaspoon vanilla essence
grated rind of 1 orange and 1 lemon

4–6 fresh peaches
2 oz flaked almonds (50 g)
3 tablespoons soft brown sugar
2 tablespoons honey
juice of 1 lemon
juice of 1 orange

In the peach season, this is good lunchtime pudding as children and adults will both enjoy it and it will avoid the squabbles over who has a peach or whose peach is the biggest. It is a cold pudding which you can make in advance but with a delicious hot syrup poured over before you serve it.

Bring the water to the boil. Put the rice in and simmer until just tender, not really soft, still with a slight nutty bite to it. Drain the rice into a large sieve and rinse through with cold water. Cool completely. Whip the cream until fairly stiff. Stir into it the castor sugar, vanilla essence, the grated rind of the orange and lemon (the juice of which you are going to use later in the sauce) and the yoghurt. Stir this cream mixture into the rice and transfer to a fairly wide, shallow serving dish. Slice the peaches thinly and arrange all over the rice mixture. Scatter flaked almonds on top of the peaches. Before serving melt the brown sugar and honey with the lemon and orange juice in a saucepan and boil quickly until it thickens. Pour all over the peaches and almonds or put into a jug and use it as a hot sauce to serve with the pudding.

Caramel Mousse

1 14 oz tin of condensed milk (400 g)
juice of 1 lemon
milk to dilute

whisked whites of 2 eggs (adult version
brandy added to taste)

Although this pudding looks and tastes quite elaborate it is a clever deceit because it is really very easy and cheap. It is popular for family lunches or with a spot of brandy can be made quite "grown up" for dinner parties! You can boil up several tins of condensed milk in advance and keep them in you store cupboard so that the pudding is then almost instant to make when you want it.

Boil the unopened tin of condensed milk in water in a covered pan for about three hours. Check the water from time to time to see that it is not boiling away. Cool. Open tin and empty the caramelised contents into a mixing bowl with the lemon juice, added gradually. Mix up well and if it is a very stiff mixture add a bit of milk until it is smooth and fairly thick. Fold in the whisked whites of egg and put into a bowl. Serve with sponge fingers or those Langues de Chats biscuits – it is very rich so I do not think you need cream. For the adult version I add a bit of brandy to taste, before folding in the whites of egg, and I sprinkle some chopped nuts on the top.

Balkan Syllabub

½ pint fruit yoghurt (275 ml)
½ pint extra thick or double cream
275 ml)
juice of ½ lemon
2 oz almond flakes (50 g)

This really is an instant pudding but very good too. It can be made with any flavour fruit yoghurt but I think apricot combines best with the cream and lemon juice.

Put the yoghurt into a mixing bowl. Stir in the lemon juice. Whip the cream and whisk thoroughly into the yoghurt. Put the mixture into individual dishes (glass ones look best). Sprinkle flaked almonds on the top and chill well in the fridge before' serving.

VARIATION
Mix plain yoghurt sweetened with castor sugar with the whisked cream and lemon juice. Put into dishes and sprinkle soft brown sugar all over the top. Chill in the fridge before serving. The brown sugar melts slightly and makes a delicious topping.

Chilled Brandy Soufflé with Hot Chocolate Sauce

½ pint milk (275 ml)
5 large eggs
4 oz castor sugar (110 g)
2 tablespoons brandy
1 teaspoon vanilla essence
½ oz gelatine (10 g)
2 oz chopped nuts (50 g)

FOR THE CHOCOLATE SAUCE
2–3 tablespoons brandy
1 full tablespoon golden syrup or honey
8 oz Chocolate Menier or plain
chocolate (225 g)
1 oz butter (25 g)

I once had something like this in a restaurant in France; it was just called "Entremet du Chef" and the waitress said it was the chef's invention. She told me it was complicated to make but as it was so delicious I was determined to find an uncomplicated way to make it, and I think I have achieved a dish as good as "Le Chef's".

Oil a loose bottomed 7 in (18 cm) cake tin. Separate the yolks from the whites of egg, putting the yolks in a large mixing bowl and the whites in a slightly smaller one. Put the milk, castor sugar, 2 tablespoons brandy and vanilla essence in with the yolks. Put the bowl over a large saucepan of simmering water and whisk the contents together for 10–15 minutes until it has thickened slightly and is very hot. Dissolve the gelatine completely in a little water in a saucepan over a low heat. Whisk the gelatine into the hot egg mixture. Let it go cold in the bowl until it just begins to set. Re-whisk briefly to make it smooth. Whisk the egg whites until stiff and fold them into the yolk mixture together with the chopped nuts. Put the mixture into the oiled cake tin and chill in the fridge until set. Turn it out of the cake tin upside down on to a serving dish and then carefully remove the loose bottom of the cake tin which will now be on top of the soufflé. Grate a little chocolate or sprinkle some nuts on the top to decorate. Keep in the fridge. In a small basin over simmering water, or in a double saucepan, melt the chocolate, broken up, with the brandy, butter and the golden syrup, and stir well together. Serve this sauce hot with the chilled soufflé. I serve a little cream with it too, the sight of it trickling over the hot chocolate sauce is very mouthwatering.

Blackcurrant Marble Mousse on a Crust

FOR THE CRUST
6 oz digestive biscuits (175 g)
1 heaped tablespoon demerara sugar
1 oz melted butter (25 g)
pinch of salt

FOR THE MOUSSE
¾–1 pint blackcurrant purée (425–570 ml)
juice of 1 lemon
1 oz gelatine (25 g)
2 egg whites
8 fl oz double cream (225 ml)
¼ pint yoghurt (150 ml)
1 tablespoon castor sugar
2 oz flaked almonds (50 g)

This mousse has a lovely marbled appearance and can be made with any good, strong-tasting fruit. It is especially delicious with purée made from stewed damsons or from stewed dried apricots. It is marbled with a mixture of cream and yogurt which gives it a fresh taste. I have suggested flaked almonds for the top which give a good crunchy contrast but of course in the summer you could arrange fresh soft fruit on the top which would look and taste even better.

Crush the biscuits in a liquidiser or with a rolling pin on a large board. Put them in a bowl and stir the sugar, salt and melted butter in thoroughly. Brush the base of a loose bottomed 7–8 in (18–20 cm) round cake tin with oil. Put the biscuit mixture into the tin and pat down firmly with the metal spoon. Put the tin in the centre of the oven Gas 5 (375°F/190°C) for 5 minutes. Take out and cool.

Stir the lemon juice into the blackcurrant purée in a saucepan. Slightly warm the purée. Dissolve the gelatine completely in a little hot water in a saucepan and stir it into the purée. Cool until just beginning to set. Whisk the egg whites until stiff and fold them gently but thoroughly into the purée. In another bowl whisk the cream until thick and stir in the castor sugar and the yoghurt. Stir this cream mixture very roughly into the purée and egg whites but do not mix together properly, leave it in streaks. Brush the sides of the cake tin with oil. Pour the purée mixture into the tin. Put in the fridge for at least an hour before turning out of the loose bottomed tin. The easiest way to do this is to put the tin on top of a jam jar and let the sides slip down. Carefully edge the crust off the base of the tin on to a serving plate. Sprinkle flaked almonds all over the top.

Chocolate Mousse Gâteau

6 oz Chocolate Menier or plain
chocolate (175 g)
5 eggs
6 oz castor sugar (175 g)
2 tablespoons very hot water
½ pint double cream (275 ml)
about ¾ lb (350 g) fresh summer fruit, or
good jam, or 8 oz (225 g) dried apricots,
stewed as above

Several friends have said that they have never tasted a better pudding than this. It is a mouthwatering soft dark chocolate sandwich cake made with just eggs, sugar and chocolate, no flour at all, and it is then packed with fruit and whipped cream. It must be made well in advance but it is not difficult and is extremely impressive and beautiful for a dinner party. In the summer, I fill it with strawberries, raspberries, redcurrants or sliced peaches. You could use blackberries in the autumn. In the winter you can use any good whole fruit jam but I usually do some stewed dried apricots which have such a sharp strong taste and are just as delicious as the summer fruit. If you do use apricots soak about 8 oz in water for a few hours and then simmer gently in a saucepan with 3 oz brown sugar, water to cover and juice of a lemon, for about ¾ hour until they go very thick. Then cool and let get very cold in the fridge before filling the cake with them. If you use fresh fruit reserve a few to decorate the top. This recipe serves about eight people.

Brush two 7–8 in (18–20 cm) sandwich tins with oil and put a disc of greaseproof paper in the bottom of each. Break the chocolate into small pieces and put over a pan of hot, but not boiling, water. Stir occasionally until it melts. Meanwhile, separate the eggs putting the yolks into a large basin and the whites into a smaller basin. Add the sugar to the yolks and whisk thoroughly together until the mixture is pale in colour and fairly thick in consistency. When the chocolate has melted remove from the heat and whisk it into the egg yolks and sugar. Whisk in 2 tablespoons of very hot water to soften the mixture. Whisk the egg whites until stiff and then fold gently but thoroughly into the chocolate mixture with a metal spoon. Heat oven to Gas 4 (350°F/180°C). Pour the mixture into the prepared sandwich tins and bake in the centre of the oven for 15–20 minutes until firm to a light touch in the middle. When you take them out they will sink down a bit – do not worry about it. Cool and then let get completely cold in the fridge for at least an hour, or overnight if you want. Have a large round plate ready. Loosen the edges of the cakes with a knife. Then turn out one cake on to the round plate. It will come quite easily with a gentle shake. Spread the fruit over the cake. If it is fresh fruit you may like to sprinkle it with castor sugar. Whisk the cream until stiff and spread it over the fruit. Then turn the second cake out on top of the cream. Keep cool. Before serving sprinkle the top all over with the icing sugar through a sieve and if you have filled it with fresh fruit put a few on the top to decorate.

Chocolate Mousse Wrapped in Cream Cheese and Hazelnuts

(serves 6–8)

12 oz full fat cream cheese (350 g)
2 tablespoons castor sugar
3 oz chopped hazelnuts (75 g) (if you buy whole ones just whizz them in a blender for a moment to chop them)

1–2 tablespoons rum, brandy or Cointreau
4 large eggs
½ oz gelatine (10 g)
2 tablespoons soft brown sugar

FOR THE CHOCOLATE MOUSSE FILLING
12 oz plain chocolate or dark cooking chocolate (350 g)
½ oz butter (10 g)

FOR THE BISCUIT BASE
6 oz (175 g) sweet crunchy type biscuits – crumbled in a liquidiser or with a rolling pin
1 oz butter (25 g)

This is a luxurious and delicious surprise pudding for a dinner party. It looks like a creamily iced cake flecked with hazelnuts but when you cut into it there is a rich fluffy chocolate mousse inside all on a crunchy biscuit base. You can prepare it well in advance. This amount will probably feed more than six people but I think you will find it gets finished up fairly quickly.

Beat together the cream cheese and castor sugar and stir in the chopped hazelnuts. Get a 7 in (18 cm) diameter fairly deep cake tin and line both the base and the sides with greaseproof paper or foil. Press and spread the cheese mixture about ¼ in (½ cm) thick over the bottom and up the sides approximately 2 in (5 cm) high. Cool in the fridge while you make the filling.

Break the chocolate into small pieces in a mixing bowl with 4 tablespoons of water. Put this bowl over a pan of gently simmering water and leave the chocolate to melt. Dissolve the gelatine and the brown sugar in a little water in a pan over a medium heat and stir into the melting chocolate. When it has melted turn the heat off and continue stirring for a few minutes and stir in the butter and rum. Remove the bowl from the pan. Separate the eggs putting the whites into a large bowl. Beat the yolks into the slightly cooled chocolate mixture. When the mixture feels almost cold whisk the egg whites until stiff and fold them gently into the chocolate mixture. Pour the mixture into the cream-cheese coating and leave to set in the fridge for an hour or more. If the cream-cheese sides come more than about ¼ in (½ cm) above the chocolate just push them down a bit. Melt the butter and stir it into the crumbled sweet biscuits. Spoon this mixture on top of the set chocolate mousse and press smoothly down with a metal spoon. Put in the fridge for another half hour or more. Turn the cake out of the tin on to a serving plate and carefully remove the greaseproof paper or foil. Grate a little chocolate on top if you like. Keep the pudding in the fridge until needed and serve with cream.

CAKES AND BISCUITS

Devil's Food Cake with American Frosting   page 126
Easy Chocolate Cake with Fresh
    Orange Fudge Frosting   127
Almond and Peel Cake   128
Orange, Apple and Apricot Honey Cake   128
Featherlight Flower Cake   129
Rum and Treacle Fruit Cake   130
Delicious Spiced Cheese Straws   131
Melt in the Mouth Biscuits   132

Devil's Food Cake with American Frosting

FOR THE CAKE
3 oz Chocolate Menier or plain chocolate (75 g)
3 tablespoons water
6 oz butter (175 g)
10½ oz soft dark brown sugar (285 g)
1 teaspoon vanilla essence
3 eggs – lightly whisked
6 fl oz milk soured by adding the juice of ½ large lemon (175 ml)
10½ oz plain flour (285 g)
¾ level teaspoon baking powder
1½ level teaspoons bicarbonate of soda (sifted together with flour and baking powder)
Good apricot, blackcurrant or black cherry jam to fill

FOR THE AMERICAN FROSTING
2 egg whites
12 oz castor sugar (350 g)
good pinch salt
3 tablespoons water
about 1 tablespoon lemon juice
½ teaspoon cream of tartar

Of course I cannot claim this beautiful cake to be my own concoction but it is so delicious, and having tried many recipes for it I have finally arrived at a combination of several which I find makes the best cake. It is a perfect cake for birthdays or parties. I even use it as a Christmas cake because after eating Christmas pudding and mince pies no one in our house seems to feel like rich fruit cake at teatime. Also the gleaming white American frosting makes such wonderful snow. It is so easy to shape into ice slopes for a skiing Father Christmas and his reindeer pulling a sledge, while perhaps a snowman sits under a frosty Christmas tree nearby and the robin redbreast sits perkily on his log! True American frosting which you make with a sugar thermometer is wonderful but not guaranteed to succeed and I find it tricky to do without the help of a second person. This mock American frosting is very good indeed and easy both to make and to ice with. It is better if you can make and ice the cake one or two days in advance.

Line 2 greased 8–9 in (20–23 cm) sandwich tins with greased greaseproof paper. Break the chocolate into small pieces and put with 3 tablespoons of water in a double saucepan or a bowl over simmering water stirring occasionally until smooth. Remove from the heat and cool slightly. Turn on the oven to Gas 4 (350°F/180°C). Cream the fat with the sugar and vanilla essence until light and fluffy. Thoroughly beat in the lightly whisked eggs and melted chocolate. Add the soured milk alternately with the flour, baking powder and bicarbonate of soda. Divide the mixture between the two tins and smooth with a knife. Bake towards the centre of the oven, which you have pre-heated to Gas 4 (350°F/180°C) for 30–40 minutes until well risen and springy to a touch in the centre. Leave in the tins for 10 minutes, then turn the cakes carefully out on to a wire tray to cool and remove the greaseproof paper. When cold sandwich together with plenty of good strong-tasting jam and ice with American frosting.

To make the frosting put all the ingredients together into a large deep bowl and whisk thoroughly together. Put the bowl over a pan of very hot water and continue to whisk for about 10 minutes until the mixture is thick enough to stand in peaks and the sugar has dissolved. Spread at once thickly all over the cake with a wide knife making rough flicks. Decorate if liked.

Easy Chocolate Cake with Fresh Orange Fudge Frosting

6 oz soft margarine (175 g)
6 oz soft brown sugar (Barbados if possible) (175 g)
1 teaspoon vanilla essence
6 oz dark chocolate, melted with a little water (175 g)

3 eggs
6 oz self-raising flour (175 g)
1 teaspoon baking powder
a little icing sugar

This is a light and very chocolatey cake. It is also used as the base for Blackcurrant and Almond Chocolate Flan on page 108.

Heat oven to Gas 3 (325°F/160°C). Butter two 7–8 in (18–20 cm) sandwich tins. In a mixing bowl whisk up the soft margarine and the sugar until light and fluffy. Add the vanilla essence and the melted chocolate and whisk in. Whisk in the eggs one by one. Stir in the flour sifted with the baking powder and whisk up for half minute. Put mixture into the sandwich tins and bake in the centre of the oven for 30–35 minutes until springy to a touch in the middle. Cool and sandwich together with the frosting. A simple alternative is a good strong-tasting blackcurrant or black cherry jam and a little sour cream too is very good. Sprinkle icing sugar through a fine sieve on to the top of the cake and decorate with grated chocolate.

FOR THE FROSTING
2 oz butter (50 g)
6 oz soft brown sugar (175 g)

grated peel and juice of 1 medium-sized orange
1 oz plain chocolate (25 g)
6 oz icing sugar (175 g)

This icing or filling is absolutely delicious when you want to make a chocolate cake more of a party cake. The icing has a very rich fudge flavour and the freshness of the orange juice stops it being sickly. This amount will fill and ice the top of a 7–8 in (18–20 cm) sandwich cake and is quick and easy to make.

Put the butter, the soft brown sugar, the orange peel and juice into a saucepan. Heat together gently, stirring, until the sugar dissolves. Remove from the heat, add the chocolate and stir until melted. Gradually stir in the icing sugar and beat until smooth. Do not fill or ice the cake until the icing has cooled enough to spread easily but not to run over the edges.

Almond and Peel Cake

4 oz butter (110 g)
5 oz castor sugar (150 g)
3 eggs – lightly beaten
3 oz ground almonds (75 g)

1½ oz plain flour (40 g)
½ teaspoon vanilla essence
2 oz candied peel (50 g)
demerara sugar to sprinkle on top

This is a delicious, moist and light cake which is quick and easy to make.

Grease and flour a fairly deep 7 in (18 cm) sandwich tin. Put a disc of greaseproof paper in the bottom. Cream the butter and sugar and the vanilla essence in a bowl until light and fluffy. Add the eggs and the ground almonds alternately. Beat well. Dust the peel with a little flour and stir lightly into the mixture. Fold in the flour with a metal spoon. Turn mixture into the tin, smooth top and sprinkle with demerara sugar. Bake in the centre of a pre-heated oven Gas 4 (350°F/180°C) for 45–50 minutes. Cool in the tin before turning out – if necessary loosen sides with a knife. I usually stick a few flaked almonds into the top of the cake to decorate.

Orange, Apple and Apricot Honey Cake

8 oz butter (225 g)
4 tablespoons honey
4 oz castor sugar (110 g)
3 teaspoons orange essence
4 eggs – lightly whisked
6 oz dried apricots – chopped small,
soaked for ½ hour in cold water and
drained (175 g)

grated rind of 1 orange (optional)
2 large cooking apples
8 oz self-raising flour (225 g)
1 teaspoon baking powder

This is a large and deliciously flavoured cake which keeps fresh and moist for several days. You should bake it in one of the loose based cake tins as it tends to stick.

Heat oven to Gas 3 (325°F/170°C). Line the bottom of a well greased, loose based 8 in (20 cm) cake tin with greased greaseproof paper. Cream the butter with the sugar and honey until light and fluffy. Add the orange essence, then the eggs a little at a time, whisking after each addition. Sift the flour with the baking powder and fold in with a metal spoon. Peel and chop up the apples into small pieces and stir them and the chopped soaked apricots into the cake mixture. (If you have an orange grate the rind and stir it in.) Put the mixture into the cake tin and bake in the centre of the oven for 1½ hours. Leave to stand for 10 minutes or so before putting a knife round the edge and gently pushing the cake out of the tin. While the cake is very hot brush the top with honey and sprinkle over a little demerara sugar.

Featherlight Flower Cake

3 large eggs
3 oz castor sugar (75 g)
a few drops of rose or violet essence (or
triple strength rose water)
3 oz plain flour (75 g)
1½ level teaspoons baking powder
pinch salt
¼ pint double cream (150 ml)
crystallised rose or violet petals —
optional

The addition of either violet or rose essence gives this fatless sponge cake a subtle and refreshing flavour. It is quick and easy to make and should really be eaten on the day it is made. But since both adults and children love it and it looks so tempting glistening under its topping of castor sugar it will probably get eaten within moments. If you like, spread a layer of redcurrant or crabapple jelly under the cream in the centre.

Grease two 7 in (18 cm) sandwich tins and line the bottoms with a disc of greased greaseproof paper. Sift the flour, baking powder and salt together two or three times and put on one side. Put the eggs and the sugar into a deep bowl over a pan of hot water and whisk with an electric or hand whisk until the mixture becomes really thick so that it retains the impression of the whisk when you pull it out. Add the rose or violet essence and whisk in. Take the bowl off the pan of hot water. Gently fold in the sifted flour with a metal spoon. Divide the mixture equally between the two sandwich tins and cook in the centre of a pre-heated oven at Gas 5 (375°F/190°C) for 15 minutes until the cakes are light brown and springy to a touch in the centre. Lay a folded teacloth on a wire cooling rack. Loosen the edges of the cakes with a knife and turn out on to the teacloth. (This avoids getting the marks of the wire rack on the cakes.) Carefully remove the greaseproof paper. When cool, whip the cream until stiff, adding a few drops of rose or violet essence to taste, and use to sandwich the cakes together. Sprinkle the top with castor sugar and decorate with crystallised rose or violet petals.

Rum and Treacle Fruit Cake

8 oz self-raising flour (225 g)
6 oz butter (175 g)
2 oz soft brown sugar (50 g)
4 tablespoons black treacle dissolved
in a cup of warm milk
8 oz raisins (225 g)
6 oz dried apricots – chopped into
small pieces (175 g)
1–2 teaspoons powdered mace or
nutmeg
2 eggs – lightly beaten
1–2 small glasses dark rum
a little clear honey, or golden syrup
a little demerara sugar
pinch salt

This crumbling moist cake, glossy and enticing, is really packed with fruit. It is very simple to make and useful to have around at weekends. If you have no dark rum use whisky, brandy or even sherry.

Grease and line a 7 in (18 cm) cake tin with greased greaseproof paper. Put the flour into a mixing bowl with a pinch of salt and sugar. Cut the butter into the flour and sugar and rub with your fingers until the mixture is free from lumps. Stir in the raisins and the chopped apricots, the peel and the spice. Pour in the beaten eggs and stir the mixture together thoroughly, and then stir in the rum and the treacle dissolved in milk. Put the mixture into the cake tin and bake in the centre of a pre-heated oven Gas 4 (350°F/180°C) for half an hour, then turn the heat down to Gas 2½ (310°F/155°C) for a further three quarters to 1 hour or until a sharp knife stuck into the centre comes out dry. Leave the cake in the tin for about 5 minutes and then turn it out on to a cooling tray. While the cake is hot brush it all over with some clear honey or golden syrup. Sprinkle a little demerara sugar on the top and leave to cool.

Delicious Spiced Cheese Straws

6 oz grated cheese (175 g)
4 oz plain wholemeal flour (110 g)
2 level teaspoons baking powder
4 teaspoons mixed spice
4 oz butter (110 g)
2 egg yolks

These are just very light, specially good cheese straws and the nutty taste of the wholemeal flour plus the spices makes them rather unusual.

Pre-heat oven to Gas 7 (425°F/220°C). Put the grated cheese into a mixing bowl. Weigh out the flour and sieve it with the baking powder and spice into the cheese. Cut the butter into small pieces and rub into the flour and cheese with your fingers. Add the egg yolks and mix with a wooden spoon into a stiff dough. Gather into a ball, press out with your hands on to a floured board and then roll to about ½ in (1 cm) thick. Cut into straws with a sharp knife and place carefully on a large ungreased baking sheet. Bake in the top part of the oven for 8–12 minutes until just golden brown. Cool and then remove carefully from the baking sheet.

VARIATIONS. You can make curried cheese straws by substituting the mixed spice with 3 teaspoons of curry powder.

Melt in the Mouth Biscuits

6 oz butter (175 g)
2 oz icing sugar (50 g)
½ lb self-raising flour (225 g)

I cannot claim this recipe as my own but these featherlight biscuits are so delicious and simple to make that I feel I must give other people the opportunity of making them. I first ate them at a nursery tea in Scotland; in a towered hilltop house under the moor. The wind screamed outside and the fire crackled and glowed in the grate. Our appetites were keen from a striding walk and the large round table was laden with griddle scones, drop scones, fluffy fatless sponges with fresh cream and strawberry jam oozing out, and a large plateful of these pale golden biscuits. I thought that it must be the magic Scottish touch, acquired after years of baking, which made the simple biscuits so good but I tried them out at home and still they really did "melt in your mouth". I have now made all sorts of variations to the basic mixture, some of which I have suggested here.

Cream the butter thoroughly with the icing sugar in a bowl. Work the flour in well with your fingers. Gather together into a ball of dough and knead slightly – if it seems sticky flour your hands. Roll out on to a floured board to about ⅛–¼ in (3 mm–½ cm) thick and cut into rounds. Re-roll as necessary. Lay the rounds on lightly greased baking sheets and bake in the centre of the oven Gas 5 (375°F/190°C) for 8–10 minutes until pale golden brown. Allow the biscuits to cool on the tray. These biscuits are perfect with fresh fruit fools in the summer.

VARIATIONS
Orange biscuits. *Add the finely grated rind of 2 oranges with the flour.*
Spicy biscuits. *Add 1–2 teaspoons powdered cinnamon or mixed spice with the flour.*
Chocolate biscuits. *Replace 1 oz flour (25 g) with 1 oz cocoa powder (25 g). If you put a blob of white icing on top they are perfect for children's parties and very delicious.*
Nut biscuits. *Add 1 oz chopped nuts (25 g) to the flour.*
Wholemeal biscuits. *Use self-raising wholemeal or wheatmeal flour instead of white flour.*

Five Lanzarote Recipes

For the last twelve years I have spent simple seaside holidays on a stark volcanic island in the Canaries where my mother has a house. The fishing village is in a barren desert, reached by driving through a sea of tumbling black lava which looks as though it bubbled out from the volcanoes yesterday. There is no electricity yet and very little water but the flat-roofed whitewashed houses dazzle in the bright sun and the beaches are what one dreams a perfect beach to be, with soft yellow sand and brilliant blue transparent sea, shot through with glinting gold reflections. It's a place to concentrate on all the reading, sleeping or swimming which one doesn't have time for at home. For me, it's also a place where I don't have to shop or cook. There is a very small, very wide lady called Maria who really likes cooking in the experimental way that I do. The variety of food available is limited, though of course the fish is good and always fresh. Maria had a dramatic life living in a derelict house on a cliff with a drunken husband who was said to break the bed and tear her clothes, and eventually fell off the roof while full of Spanish brandy, and left her with six little children to support. She has never learnt to read or write and can't follow recipes, but the dishes she concocts are always good and eaten by all of us with great enthusiasm. Here are a few of them.

FIRST COURSE

Goats' Cheese Salad with Garbonzas   page   134

MAIN COURSE

Squid and Tomato Paella   135
Lanzarote Cassoulet   136
Baked Spiced Fish   137
Maria's Fish Albondigas with Devilled Tomato
    Sauce   138

Goats' Cheese Salad with Garbonzas

**6 oz dried chick peas – soaked
overnight in water (175 g)
2 small onions
6–8 oz Feta goats' cheese (175–225 g)
1 lb tomatoes (450 g)
fresh basil leaves, chopped or 2
tablespoons dried oregano
vinaigrette dressing made with one
third wine vinegar (or vinegar and
lemon juice), salt, a lot of black pepper,
1 clove garlic crushed, two thirds olive
oil**

Halfway up a volcano behind the village there is a very quiet, polite lady in a neat little house who has a herd of well kept goats and makes cheese. Three plump girls work at the cheese in a hut next to the house. It is rather like the Greek Feta cheese and is delicious when it is very fresh and moist. I usually buy a large cheese on my last day there and bring it back to my freezer, cut into portions, so that we can always have the really fresh taste of it. I made a salad with it as a first course, adding chick peas which I urge people to use more because I think they are one of the best of the dried beans. You have to remember to soak them for several hours or overnight in water but otherwise they are very easy. If you can get fresh basil for this dish it makes a wonderful difference, but otherwise use dried oregano.

Rinse the soaked chick peas and cook them in some salted simmering water for about 15–45 minutes (the cooking time depends on the age and quality of the chick peas) – you must test them often as they should be just soft but not left to go mushy. Drain and cool. Slice the onions very finely, slice the tomatoes and cut the Feta cheese up into small chunks. Mix all together with the chick peas in a large shallow dish or bowl. Sprinkle chopped basil or oregano all over – mix up the dressing with a fork, pour it all over the salad and serve. If you can get Greek or Indian bread it is good with this, or else good wholemeal bread.

Squid and Tomato Paella

1 large cup rice
2½ cups water
pinch of saffron (or 1 teaspoon
turmeric)
salt
1 lb squid (450 g)
4–5 tomatoes – peeled and chopped
small
1 tablespoon dried oregano (or fresh
basil chopped)
2 cloves garlic – crushed
black pepper, salt
olive oil, butter

My children's favourite Lanzarote meal is little curly bits of squid, or baby octopus dipped in beaten egg and deep fried in oil. For them squid and chips for lunch is a high spot of the holiday! This simple squid and tomato paella is also very good. Maria always uses dried oregano but if you can get fresh basil it is delicious.

Boil the rice in salted water with the saffron or turmeric until the rice is just tender but not too soft. Transfer to a large sieve and rinse thoroughly with hot water. Put into a fairly large round but shallow serving dish and fork in some dots of butter. Keep warm in a low oven, covered with foil. Cut the head off the squid and extract the transparent bone. Cut the body and tentacles up into small pieces. Fry gently in a large pan for about 10 minutes in some olive oil and butter until tender – add the peeled chopped tomatoes and fry for about 3–4 minutes more. Stir in the garlic and herbs, salt and black pepper. Add this mixture to the rice and serve with a green salad.

Lanzarote Cassoulet

1 lb boneless stewing pork or lamb
(450 g)
½ lb piece smoked streaky bacon (225 g)
½–¾ lb dried chick peas (225–350 g)
1 large red or green pepper – chopped
4 large tomatoes – quartered
2–3 large cloves garlic – peeled and
chopped
1 tablespoon oregano or fresh
marjoram
1 glass white wine
olive oil
salt, black pepper

This is a lovely stew rather like a cassoulet which Maria cooks for lunch, after which we all, including the children, sink into a particularly deep siesta sleep. She uses chick peas instead of haricot beans and always puts peppers in and plenty of garlic. She occasionally puts in bits of the Spanish sausage called Chorizo and you could add coarse salami-type sausage if you liked. She usually serves it with a very good salad of tomato and a lot of raw onion. You must soak the chick peas in water for at least an hour first.

Chop the meat up into chunks. Cut the rind off the bacon and chop into chunks. Fry meat and bacon in a little olive oil until brown on all sides. Put in a casserole with the chopped pepper and tomatoes, the garlic, the soaked chick peas, the oregano, plenty of black pepper, a little salt, the wine and enough water to almost cover the ingredients. Put the covered dish in a hot oven Gas 8 (450°F/230°C) for about 15 minutes and then turn heat down to Gas 3 (325°F/160°C) for about 1½ hours.

Baked Spiced Fish

1 whole fish – about 2–3 lb gutted but
with the head left on (900 g–1 kg 350 g)
2 teaspoons powdered cumin
3 teaspoons curry powder
1 dessertspoon oregano
2 large cloves garlic – peeled and
roughly chopped
1 large or 2 small lemons
small glass white wine or dry sherry
2–3 large tomatoes
salt, black pepper
butter
a little olive oil

This is a very delicious way of cooking a large whole fish. In Lanzarote it is usually grey mullet which you can get here from a good fishmonger. You could use bream or, if you can get it, fresh sea bass is a really superior fish. The flavour of the spices and the lemon sinks into the fish and gives this easy dish a very special taste, and the juice which comes from it is wonderful.

Butter a piece of foil large enough to wrap the fish in. Sprinkle cumin, curry powder and oregano, a little black pepper and salt all over the fish. Put the chopped garlic inside where the fish has been gutted. Lay the fish on the foil. Cut the lemon and tomatoes into round slices and arrange under and on top of the fish. Pour over the wine and a little olive oil and wrap up the fish completely with foil and put on a roasting pan or baking tray. Bake in a fairly hot oven Gas 6 (400°F/200°C) for three quarters of an hour. Unwrap the foil, being careful not to let the juice spill out. Gently and carefully push the fish off the foil on to a large serving dish, arranging the tomatoes and the lemon on top of the fish. If there is room the juice can be poured round the fish, otherwise pour it into a separate jug. Plain boiled potatoes are good with this to mop up the lovely juice.

Maria's Fish Albondigas with Devilled Tomato Sauce

about ½–¾ lb cooked boned fish (or chicken) (225–350 g)
2 onions – grated
good pinch of saffron or 1 teaspoon turmeric
2 heaped tablespoons plain flour
1 teaspoon grated nutmeg
2 eggs – beaten
3 oz butter (75 g)

oil or fat to fry in
about 1 pint warm milk (570 ml)

FOR THE SAUCE TO GO WITH THEM
¾ lb tomatoes (350 g)
1 teaspoon chilli powder
1–2 tablespoons wine vinegar
salt

There are always little bits of leftover cooked fish about so we often have these "albon-digas" which are like very light fish cakes. They can be made a crisp golden outside and should be very soft and almost melt in the mouth inside. They are a good lunch or supper dish with a salad. The first part of the preparation must be done at least two hours beforehand. The tomato sauce is cold and can be made in advance.

Melt about 2 oz butter (50 g) and fry the grated onion gently until transparent in a large deep frying pan. Melt in an extra ounce or so of butter, add the flaked fish and just stir and coat the fish with butter. Take away from the heat. Stir in the flour. Put the saffron, or turmeric, the nutmeg, salt and plenty of black pepper into the milk in a saucepan and heat. Pour the milk gradually on to the fish and onions and stir thoroughly. Bring slowly to simmering and simmer gently stirring often until the mixture is thick. It should be like a soft dough – if it looks terribly stiff stir in some more warm milk, or if it is too liquid add about a dessertspoon of flour blended in a little milk, and bring up to the boil again. Put the mixture in the fridge for at least 2 hours. Flour a board and your hands and make the cold mixture into small rissole shapes. Roll them in the flour. Have the beaten egg ready. Heat up some smoking hot oil or fat in the frying pan (the oil should be about ½ in /1 cm deep or more), dip each albondiga in the beaten egg then fry them quite fast until golden brown. Take them out of the fat on a slotted spoon and drain the excess fat off by putting the albondigas on to a piece of paper kitchen roll before arranging them in a serving dish.

FOR THE SAUCE TO GO WITH THEM
Skin the tomatoes by first dipping them for a minute in boiling water then transferring them to cold water. Either mash up well with a fork, put through a Mouli or put in a liquidiser with the other ingredients. This sauce is to put on the side of your plate to dip the "albondigas" into.

Index

ALMONDS
Almond and Onion Chilli Puff, 33
Almond and Peel Cake, 128
Blackcurrant and Almond Chocolate Flan, 108
Balkan Syllabub, 120
Blackcurrant Marble Mousse on a Crust, 122
Brussels Sprouts with Almond and Nutmeg Cream, 91
Chicken Breasts and Almonds in Creamy Cheese Sauce, 81
Chilled Spinach Soup with Almonds, 12
Cream Cheese Shortbread Flan, 114
Creamy Rice with Peaches, 119
Stuffed Fillets of Plaice, 45

ALMONDS: GROUND
Autumn Pie with Almond Crust, 110
Blackcurrant and Almond Chocolate Flan, 108
Eggs with Almond and Spring Onion Stuffing, 32

ANCHOVIES
Stripy Fish Fillets in Lemon Dressing, 20

APPLES
Apple with Special Meringue, 102
Apricot Apples Baked with Rum, 103
Autumn Pie with Almond Crust, 110
Cashew Nut Fruit Pie, 109
Chicken Coriander Pie with Cider and Mustard, 69
Dittisham Casserole, 59
Orange Apple and Apricot Honey Cake, 128

APRICOTS: DRIED
Apricot Apples Baked with Rum, 103
Apricot and Sour Cream Tart with Orange Pastry, 113
Orange Apple and Apricot Honey Cake, 128
Rum and Treacle Fruit Cake, 138
Autumn Pie with Almond Crust, 110

AVOCADOS
Avocados with Cockles and Mussels, 27
Deep Sea Tart, 22

BACON
Hearty Beef Casserole, 57
Lanzarote Cassoulet, 136
Pigeon Pie, 70
Special Terrine of Rabbit with Prunes, 34–5
Stuffed Fillets of Plaice, 45
Baked Spiced Fish, 137
Balkan Syllabub, 120

BEANS: BROAD
Devilled Pork Balls with Broad Beans, 28
Quick Bean Salad, 94

BEAN SPROUTS
Primrose Salad, 92

BEEF
Braised Steak in Sherry with Mushrooms, 56
Hearty Beef Casserole, 57
Meat Loaf with Pumpkin, 74
Oriental Pie, 65
Putney Pancake Parcel, 75
Rich Glazed Joint of Brisket, 48
Special Shepherd's Pie, 64

BEETROOT
Fillets of Cod in Rich Beetroot Sauce, 42

BISCUITS
Melt in the Mouth Biscuits, 132

BISCUIT BASE
Blackcurrant Marble Mousse on a Crust, 122
Chocolate Mousse Wrapped in Cream Cheese and Hazelnuts, 124
Strawberry or Raspberry Cheesecake, 107

BLACKBERRIES
Autumn Pie with Almond Crust, 110
Tropical Fruit Salad, 99

BLACKCURRANTS
Blackcurrant and Almond Chocolate Flan, 108
Blackcurrant Marble Mousse on a Crust, 122
Cashew Nut Fruit Pie, 109
Braised Steak in Sherry with Mushrooms 56

BRANDY
Brandy Spice Ice Cream with Hot Cranberry Sauce, 118
Caramel Mousse, 119
Chilled Brandy Soufflé with Hot Chocolate Sauce, 121
Sautéed Kidneys in Brandy and Orange Sauce, 85
Special Terrine of Rabbit with Prunes, 34–5

BREAD
Curried Egg Loaf, 30
Special Tomato Salad, 93
Summer Loaf, 101
Breast of Chicken Stuffed with Smoked Fish in a Mushroom and Prawn Sauce, 80
Brussels Sprouts with Almonds and Nutmeg Cream, 91

CABBAGE
Stuffed Cabbage Leaves with Dill Seeds, 77

CAKES
Almond and Peel Cake, 128
Devil's Food Cake with American Frosting, 126
Easy Chocolate Cake with Fresh Orange Fudge Frosting, 127
Featherlight Flower Cake, 129
Orange Apple and Apricot Honey Cake, 128
Rum and Treacle Fruit Cake, 130
Calves' Liver with Gooseberry Sauce, 86

CAPERS
Calves' Liver with Gooseberry Sauce, 86
Mackerel en Papillote with Tarragon and Caper Sauce, 38
Caramel Mousse, 119

CARROTS
Carrot, Hazelnut and Watercress Salad, 93
Chicken Coriander Pie with Cider and Mustard, 69
Hearty Beef Casserole, 57
Pigeon Pie, 70
Rich Glazed Joint of Brisket, 48
Swede and Carrot Soup, 13
Cashew Nut Fruit Pie, 109

CAVIARE: DANISH
Eggs Stuffed with Caviare and Cream Cheese, 31
Cheating Ice Cream with Hot Rum Sauce, 117

CHEESE
Chicken Breasts and Almonds in Creamy Cheese Sauce, 81
Chicken and Nutmeg Lasagne, 82
Delicious Spiced Cheese Straws, 131
Kidney Layer Pie, 71
Mussels Gratinée, 44
Scallops and Prawns in Garlic Cheese Sauce with Sesame Top, 39
Souffléed Fish Pie, 45
Special Shepherd's Pie, 64
Spinach Wrapped Fish Fillets in Pastry Parcels, 41
Stuffed Veal in a Pastry Case, 67
Veal Slices with Sage and Parsley, 76

CHEESE: CREAM
Cheese Apples, 115
Chocolate Mousse Wrapped in Cream Cheese and Hazelnuts, 124
Cream Cheese Shortbread Flan, 114
Curried Egg Loaf, 30
Eggs and Onion in Curried Cream Cheese Sauce, 31
Eggs Stuffed with Caviare and Cream Cheese, 31
Kipper Pâté, 35
Raspberries Wrapped in Creamed Cottage Cheese in a Crisp Meringue Case, 100
Smoked Mackerel Fillets with Smoked Cod's Roe Sauce, 21
Strawberry or Raspberry Cheesecake, 107
Summer Loaf, 101
Turmeric Pies, 24

CHEESE: GOATS
Goats' Cheese Salad with Garbonzas, 134
Cheese Apples, 115

CHICKEN
  Breasts of Chicken Stuffed with Smoked Fish in a Mushroom and Prawn Sauce, 80
  Chicken Breasts and Almonds in Creamy Cheese Sauce, 81
  Chicken Coriander Pie with Cider and Mustard, 69
  Chicken and Nutmeg Lasagne, 82
  Joints of Chicken Baked with Cinnamon, 60
  Stuffed Boned Chicken en Croûte, 68
CHICK PEAS
  Goats' Cheese Salad with Garbonzas, 134
  Lanzarote Cassoulet, 136
Chilled Brandy Soufflé with Hot Chocolate Sauce, 121
Chilled Spinach Soup with Almonds, 12
CHOCOLATE
  Blackcurrant and Almond Chocolate Flan, 108
  Cheating Ice Cream with Hot Rum Sauce, 117
  Chilled Brandy Soufflé with Hot Chocolate Sauce, 121
  Chocolate Mousse Gâteau, 123
  Chocolate Mousse Wrapped in Cream Cheese and Hazelnuts, 124
  Devil's Food Cake with American Frosting, 126
  Easy Chocolate Cake with Fresh Orange Fudge Frosting, 127
CIDER
  Chicken Coriander Pie with Cider and Mustard, 69
  Dittisham Casserole, 59
  Honeyed Pork with Raisins, 50
COCKLES
  Avocados with Cockles and Mussels, 27
COD
  Breasts of Chicken Stuffed with Smoked Fish in a Mushroom and Prawn Sauce, 80
  Fillets of Cod in Rich Beetroot Sauce, 42
  Souffléed Fish Pie, 45
COD'S ROE
  Smoked Mackerel Fillets with Smoked Cod's Roe Sauce, 21
Cold (or hot) Curried Fish Soup, 14
Cold Spiced Ham Baked in Black Treacle, 87
Cold Stuffed Red Peppers à l'Indienne, 29
COLEY
  Cold (or hot) Curried Fish Soup, 14
CRANBERRY
  Brandy Spice Ice Cream with Hot Cranberry Sauce, 118
CREAM: DOUBLE
  Avocados with Cockles and Mussels, 27
  Balkan Syllabub, 120
  Blackcurrant Marble Mousse on a Crust, 122
  Brandy Spice Ice Cream with Hot Cranberry Sauce, 118
  Cheese Apples, 115
  Chocolate Mousse Gâteau, 123
  Cream Cheese Shortbread Flan, 114
  Creamy Kirsch Dessert, 116
  Creamy Rice with Peaches, 119
  Deep Sea Tart, 22
  Featherlight Flower Cake, 129
  Fresh Orange Jelly with Flower Water Cream, 116
  Raspberries Wrapped in Creamed Cottage Cheese in a Crisp Meringue Case, 100
  Root Vegetables with Cream and Watercress, 91
  Rose Petal Tart, 105
  Rose and Rosemary Junket, 115
CREAM: SINGLE
  Breasts of Chicken Stuffed with Smoked Fish in a Mushroom and Prawn Sauce, 80
  Brussels Sprouts with Almonds and Nutmeg Cream, 91
  Chilled Spinach Soup with Almonds, 12
  Cold (or hot) Curried Fish Soup, 14
  Fillets of Cod in Rich Beetroot Sauce, 42
  Halibut Soup with Pernod, 12

Kipper and Tomato Soup, 13
Mackerel en Papillote with Tarragon and Caper Sauce, 38
Mushroom and Mustard Soup, 15
Noodles with Seafood and Garlic Sauce, 40
Sautéed Kidneys in Brandy and Orange Sauce, 85
Smoked Mackerel Fillets with Smoked Cod's Roe Sauce, 21
Stuffed Fillets of Plaice, 45
Swede and Carrot Soup, 13
Turnip and Spring Onion Soup, 15
Veal Slices with Sage and Parsley, 76
CREAM: SOURED
  Apricot and Sour Cream Tart with Orange Pastry, 113
  Braised Steak in Sherry with Mushrooms, 56
  Chicken Breasts and Almonds in Creamy Cheese Sauce, 81
  Chicken Coriander Pie with Cider and Mustard, 69
  Crunchy Layered Strawberry Tart, 104
  Marinated Lamb Fillets with Cumin, 78
  Nettle Soup, 16
  Turmeric Pies, 24
CREAM: WHIPPING
  Cheating Ice Cream with Hot Rum Sauce, 117
  Summer Fruit on Yoghurt and Whipped Cream with Hard Sugar Top, 99
  Cream Cheese Shortbread Flan, 114
CREAMED COCONUT
  Roast Pheasants with Curried Mushroom Sauce, 53
  Creamy Blanquette of Rabbit with Mustard, 61
  Creamy Kirsch Dessert, 116
  Creamy Rice with Peaches, 119
  Crunchy Layered Strawberry Tart, 104
CURRY
  Cold (or hot) Curried Fish Soup, 14
  Curried Baskets Filled with Mushrooms in Mayonnaise, 25
  Curried Egg Loaf, 30
  Eggs and Onion in Curried Cream Cheese Sauce, 31
  Oriental Pie, 65
  Quick Curried Sauce for Cold Chicken or Turkey, 88
  Roast Pheasants with Curried Mushroom Sauce, 53
Deep Sea Tart, 22
Delicious Spiced Cheese Straws, 131
Devilled Pork Balls with Broad Beans, 28
Devil's Food Cake with American Frosting, 126
Dittisham Casserole, 59
DRESSINGS
  French Dressing, 95
  Lemon Dressing for Stripy Fish Fillets, 20
  Tarragon Dressing for a Lettuce Salad, 95
Easy Chocolate Cake with Fresh Orange Fudge Frosting, 127
EGGS
  Chilled Brandy Soufflé with Hot Chocolate Sauce, 121
  Chocolate Mousse Gâteau, 123
  Chocolate Mousse Wrapped in Cream Cheese and Hazelnuts, 124
  Curried Egg Loaf, 30
  Eggs and Onion in Curried Cream Cheese Sauce, 31
  Eggs Stuffed with Caviare and Cream Cheese, 31
  Eggs with Almond and Spring Onion Stuffing, 32
  Souffléed Fish Pie, 45
  Surprise Custard Marrows, 26
Fillets of Cod in Rich Beetroot Sauce, 42
FISH
  Avocados with Cockles and Mussels, 27
  Baked Spiced Fish, 137
  Breasts of Chicken Stuffed with Smoked Fish in a Mushroom and Prawn Sauce, 80

Cold (or hot) Curried Fish Soup, 14
Deep Sea Tart, 22
Fillets of Cod in Rich Beetroot Sauce, 42
Halibut Soup with Pernod, 12
Kipper Pâté, 35
Kipper and Tomato Soup, 13
Mackerel en Papillote with Tarragon and Caper Sauce, 38
Maria's Fish Albondigas with Devilled Tomato Sauce, 138
Mediterranean Fish Casserole, 43
Mussels Gratinée, 44
Noodles with Seafood and Garlic Sauce, 40
Scallops and Prawns in Garlic Cheese Sauce with Sesame Top, 39
Smoked Mackerel Fillets with Smoked Cod's Roe Sauce, 21
Smoked Mackerel Quiche, 46
Souffléed Fish Pie, 45
Spiced Sesame Fish Bites, 23
Spinach-wrapped Fish Fillets in Pastry Parcels, 41
Squid and Tomato Paella, 135
Stripy Fish Fillets in Lemon Dressing, 20
Stuffed Fillets of Plaice, 45
FLOWER WATER: ORANGE
  Fresh Orange Jelly with Flower Water Cream, 116
FLOWER WATER: ROSE
  Creamy Kirsch Dessert, 116
  Featherlight Flower Cake, 129
  Raspberries Wrapped in Creamed Cottage Cheese in a Crisped Meringue Case, 100
  Rose Petal Tart, 105
  Rose and Rosemary Junket, 115
  Tropical Fruit Salad, 99
French Dressing, 95
Fresh Fruit Pudding, 101
Fresh Orange Jelly with Flower Water Cream, 116
Fresh Raspberry and Redcurrant Tart, 106
FROSTING
  American Frosting for Devil's Food Cake, 126
  Fresh Orange Fudge Frosting for Easy Chocolate Cake, 127
Goats' Cheese Salad with Garbonzas, 134
GOOSEBERRY
  Calves' Liver with Gooseberry Sauce, 86
  Cashew Nut Fruit Pie, 109
GUAVAS
  Tropical Fruit Salad, 99
Halibut Soup with Pernod, 12
HAM
  Cold Spiced Ham Baked in Black Treacle, 87
  Souffléed Fish Pie, 45
HAZELNUTS
  Carrot, Hazelnut and Watercress Salad, 93
  Chocolate Mousse Wrapped in Cream Cheese and Hazelnuts, 124
HEART
  Hearty Beef Casserole, 57
HONEY
  Creamy Blanquette of Rabbit with Mustard, 61
  Creamy Rice with Peaches, 119
  Honeyed Pork with Raisins, 50
  Orange Apple and Apricot Honey Cake, 128
  Rum and Treacle Fruit Cake, 130
  Stripy Fish Fillets in Lemon Dressing, 20
ICE CREAM
  Brandy Spice Ice Cream with Hot Cranberry Sauce, 118
  Cheating Ice Cream with Hot Rum Sauce, 117
JELLY
  Fresh Orange Jelly with Flower Water Cream, 116
Joints of Chicken Baked with Cinnamon, 60
JUNKET
  Rose and Rosemary Junket, 115

KIDNEY
Kidney Layer Pie, 71
Pigeon Pie, 70
Sautéed Kidneys in Brandy and Orange Sauce, 85
KIPPERS
Kipper Pâté, 35
Kipper and Tomato Soup, 13
KIRSCH
Creamy Kirsch Dessert, 116
LAMB
Cold Stuffed Red Peppers à l'Indienne, 29
Lamb Fillets with Mint, 59
Marinated Lamb Fillets with Cumin, 78
Roast Leg of Lamb with Cardamom Sauce, 51
Roast Saddle of Lamb with Southern Herb Sauce, 52
Lanzarote Cassoulet, 136
LASAGNE
Chicken and Nutmeg Lasagne, 82
LIVER
Calves' Liver with Gooseberry Sauce, 86
LYCHEES
Tropical Fruit Salad, 99
Macaroni in Mayonnaise, 94
Mackerel en Papillote with Tarragon and Caper Sauce, 38
Maria's Fish Albondigas with Devilled Tomato Sauce, 138
Marinated Lamb Fillets with Cumin, 78
MARROW
Surprise Custard Marrows, 26
MAYONNAISE
Avocados with Cockles and Mussels, 27
Curried Baskets Filled with Mushrooms in Mayonnaise, 25
Macaroni in Mayonnaise, 94
Meat Loaf with Pumpkin, 74
Mediterranean Fish Casserole, 43
Melt in the Mouth Biscuits, 132
MERINGUE
Apple with Special Meringue, 102
Old fashioned Nursery Delight, 117
Raspberries Wrapped in Creamed Cottage Cheese in a Crisp Meringue Case, 100
MILK: SWEETENED CONDENSED
Caramel Mousse, 119
MOUSSE
Blackcurrant Marble Mousse on a Crust, 122
Caramel Mousse, 119
Chocolate Mousse Gâteau, 123
Chocolate Mousse Wrapped in Cream Cheese and Hazelnuts, 124
MUSHROOMS
Braised Steak in Sherry with Mushrooms, 56
Breasts of Chicken Stuffed with Smoked Fish in a Mushroom and Prawn Sauce, 80
Chicken Breasts and Almonds in Creamy Cheese Sauce, 81
Chicken Coriander Pie with Cider and Mustard, 69
Chicken and Nutmeg Lasagne, 82
Creamy Blanquette of Rabbit with Mustard, 61
Curried Baskets Filled with Mushrooms in Mayonnaise, 25
Dittisham Casserole, 59
Mushrooms and Mint, 26
Mushroom and Mustard Soup, 15
Noodles with Seafood and Garlic Sauce, 40
Putney Pancake Parcel, 75
Ratatouille in a Veal Case, 66
Roast Pheasants with Curried Mushroom Sauce, 53
Scallops and Prawns in Garlic Cheese Sauce with Sesame Top, 39
Stuffed Boned Chicken en Croûte, 68
Stuffed Fillets of Plaice, 45
Sweetbread Risotto, 84
MUSSELS
Avocados with Cockles and Mussels, 27
Mussels Gratinée, 44

MUSTARD
Chicken Coriander Pie with Cider and Mustard, 69
Creamy Blanquette of Rabbit with Mustard, 61
Eggs with Almond and Spring Onion Stuffing, 32
Mackerel en Papillote with Tarragon and Caper Sauce, 38
Mushroom and Mustard Soup, 15
Ratatouille in a Veal Case, 66
Rich Glazed Joint of Brisket, 48
Roast Juniper Veal and Special Tomato Sauce, 49
Roast Leg of Lamb with Cardamom Sauce, 51
Smoked Mackerel Quiche, 46
Stripy Fish Fillets in Lemon Dressing, 20
Nettle Soup, 16
Noodles with Seafood and Garlic Sauce, 40
OFFAL
Calves' Liver with Gooseberry Sauce, 86
Hearty Beef Casserole, 57
Kidney Layer Pie, 71
Sautéed Kidneys in Brandy and Orange Sauce, 85
Sweetbread Risotto, 84
Old fashioned Nursery Delight, 117
ONIONS
Almond and Onion Chilli Puff, 33
Calves' Liver with Gooseberry Sauce, 86
Chicken Coriander Pie with Cider and Mustard, 69
Dittisham Casserole, 59
Eggs and Onion in Curried Cream Cheese Sauce, 31
Goats' Cheese Salad with Garbonzas, 134
Hearty Beef Casserole, 57
Kidney Layer Pie, 71
Maria's Fish Albondigas with Devilled Tomato Sauce, 138
Marinated Lamb Fillets with Cumin, 78
Meat Loaf with Pumpkin, 74
Mushrooms and Mint, 26
Putney Pancake Parcel, 75
Ratatouille in a Veal Case, 66
Rich Glazed Joint of Brisket, 48
Sautéed Kidneys in Brandy and Orange Sauce, 85
Smoked Mackerel Quiche, 46
Special Shepherd's Pie, 64
Special Tomato Salad, 93
Sweetbread Risotto, 84
Water Melon Salad, 92
ONIONS: SPRING
Eggs with Almond and Spring Onion Stuffing, 32
Turnip and Spring Onion Soup, 16
ORANGE
Apricot Apples Baked with Rum, 103
Apricot and Sour Cream Tart with Orange Pastry, 113
Cheating Ice Cream with Hot Rum Sauce, 117
Creamy Rice with Peaches, 119
Easy Chocolate Cake with Fresh Orange Fudge Frosting, 127
Fresh Orange Jelly with Flower Water Cream, 116
Joints of Chicken Baked with Cinnamon, 60
Orange Apple and Apricot Honey Cake, 128
Sautéed Kidneys in Brandy and Orange Sauce, 85
Oriental Pie, 65
PAELLA
Squid and Tomato Paella, 135
PANCAKES
Putney Pancake Parcel, 75
PASSION FRUIT
Tropical Fruit Salad, 99
PASTRY
Apricot and Sour Cream Tart with Orange Pastry, 113
Autumn Pie with Almond Crust, 110

Cashew Nut Fruit Pie, 109
Chicken Coriander Pie with Cider and Mustard, 69
Deep Sea Tart, 22
Rose Petal Tart, 105
Smoked Mackerel Quiche, 46
Turmeric Pies, 24
PASTRY: CURRY
Curried Baskets filled with Mushrooms in Mayonnaise, 25
Delicious Spiced Cheese Straws, 131
PASTRY: PUFF
Almond and Onion Chilli Puff, 33
Pigeon Pie, 70
Rose Petal Tart, 105
Spinach Wrapped Fish Fillets in Pastry Parcels, 41
Stuffed Boned Chicken en Croûte, 68
Stuffed Veal in a Pastry Case, 67
PASTRY: SHORTBREAD
Cream Cheese Shortbread Flan, 114
PÂTÉ
Kipper Pâté, 35
PEACHES
Creamy Rice with Peaches, 119
PEPPERS
Cold Stuffed Red Peppers à l'Indienne, 29
Lanzarote Cassoulet, 136
Mediterranean Fish Casserole, 43
Ratatouille in a Veal Case, 66
Scallops and Prawns in Garlic Cheese Sauce with Sesame Top, 39
Stuffed Fillets of Plaice, 45
Sweetbread Risotto, 84
PERNOD
Halibut Soup with Pernod, 12
PHEASANT
Roast Pheasants with Curried Mushroom Sauce, 53
Pigeon Pie, 70
PLAICE
Spiced Sesame Fish Bites, 23
Stuffed Fillets of Plaice, 45
PORK
Cold Spiced Ham Baked in Black Treacle, 87
Devilled Pork Balls with Broad Beans, 28
Dittisham Casserole, 59
Honeyed Pork with Raisins, 50
Lanzarote Cassoulet, 136
Pork Seed Cakes, 77
Special Terrine of Rabbit with Prunes, 34-5
Stuffed Cabbage Leaves with Dill Seeds, 77
PORRIDGE OATS
Crunchy Layered Strawberry Tart, 104
Meat Loaf with Pumpkin, 74
POTATOES
Kidney Layer Pie, 71
Pork Seed Cakes, 77
Really Good Roast Potatoes, 90
Special Shepherd's Pie, 64
Tomato and Sorrel Soup with Lovage, 17
Turnip and Spring Onion Soup, 15
PRAWNS
Breasts of Chicken Stuffed with Smoked Fish in a Mushroom and Prawn Sauce, 80
Cold (or hot) Curried Fish Soup, 14
Deep Sea Tart, 22
Mediterranean Fish Casserole, 43
Noodles with Seafood and Garlic Sauce, 40
Scallops and Prawns in Garlic Cheese Sauce with Sesame Top, 39
Stuffed Fillets of Plaice, 45
Primrose Salad, 92
PRUNES
Special Terrine of Rabbit with Prunes, 34–5
PUMPKIN
Meat Loaf with Pumpkin, 74
Putney Pancake Parcel, 75
Quick Bean Salad, 94
Quick Curried Sauce for Cold Chicken and Turkey, 88

RABBIT
  Creamy Blanquette of Rabbit with Mustard, 61
  Special Terrine of Rabbit with Prunes, 34–5
RAISINS
  Cream Cheese Shortbread Flan, 114
  Honeyed Pork with Raisins, 50
  Rum and Treacle Fruit Cake, 130
RASPBERRY
  Creamy Kirsch Dessert, 116
  Fresh Raspberry and Redcurrant Tart, 106
  Raspberries Wrapped in Creamed Cottage Cheese in a Crisp Meringue Case, 100
  Strawberry or Raspberry Cheesecake, 107
  Summer Loaf, 101
Ratatouille in a Veal Case, 66
Really Good Roast Potatoes, 90
REDCURRANT
  Raspberry and Redcurrant Tart, 106
REDCURRANT JELLY
  Blackcurrant and Almond Chocolate Flan, 108
  Crunchy Layered Strawberry Tart, 104
  Fresh Fruit Pudding, 101
  Raspberry and Redcurrant Tart, 106
  Strawberry or Raspberry Cheesecake, 107
  Summer Loaf, 101
RHUBARB
  Fresh Fruit Pudding, 101
  Old fashioned Nursery Delight, 117
RICE
  Cold Stuffed Red Peppers à l'Indienne, 29
  Squid and Tomato Paella, 135
  Sweetbread Risotto, 84
RICE: GROUND
  Creamy Kirsch Dessert, 116
RICE: PUDDING
  Creamy Rice with Peaches, 119
  Rich Glazed Joint of Brisket, 48
  Roast Juniper Veal and Special Tomato Sauce, 49
  Roast Leg of Lamb with Cardamom Sauce, 51
  Roast Pheasants with Curried Mushroom Sauce, 53
  Roast Saddle of Lamb with Southern Herb Sauce, 52
Root Vegetables with Cream and Watercress, 91
Rose Petal Tart, 105
Rose and Rosemary Junket, 115
RUM
  Apricot Apples Baked with Rum, 103
  Cheating Ice Cream with Hot Rum Sauce, 117
  Chocolate Mousse Wrapped in Cream Cheese and Hazelnuts 124
  Rum and Treacle Fruit Cake, 130
  Tropical Fruit Salad, 99
SALAD
  Carrot, Hazelnut and Watercress Salad, 93
  Goats' Cheese Salad with Garbonzas, 134
  Primrose Salad, 92
  Quick Bean Salad, 94
  Water Melon Salad, 92
SAUCE
  Brandy and Orange Sauce for Sautéed Kidneys, 85
  Cardamom Sauce for Roast Leg of Lamb, 51
  Creamy Cheese Sauce for Chicken Breasts and Almonds, 81
  Curried Cream Cheese Sauce for Eggs and Onion, 31
  Curried Mushroom Sauce for Roast Pheasants, 53
  Devilled Tomato Sauce for Maria's Fish Albondigas, 138
  Garlic Cheese Sauce for Scallops and Prawns with Sesame Top, 39
  Gooseberry Sauce for Calves' Liver, 86
  Hot Chocolate Sauce for Chilled Brandy, Soufflé, 121
  Hot Cranberry Sauce for Brandy Spice Ice Cream, 118
  Hot Rum Sauce for Cheating Ice Cream, 117

  Mushroom and Prawn Sauce for Breasts of Chicken Stuffed with Smoked Fish, 80
  Quick Curried Sauce for Cold Chicken or Turkey, 88
  Rich Beetroot Sauce for Fillets of Cod, 42
  Seafood and Garlic Sauce for Noodles, 40
  Smoked Cod's Roe Sauce for Smoked Mackerel Fillets, 21
  Sour Cream Sauce for Turmeric Pies, 24
  Southern Herb Sauce for Roast Saddle of Lamb, 52
  Special Tomato Sauce for Roast Juniper Veal, 49
  Tarragon and Caper Sauce for Mackerel en Papillote, 38
  White Sauce for Chicken and Nutmeg Lasagne, 82
Sautéed Kidneys in Brandy and Orange Sauce, 85
Scallops and Prawns in Garlic Cheese Sauce with Sesame Top, 39
SHERRY
  Braised Steak in Sherry with Mushrooms, 56
  Calves' Liver with Gooseberry Sauce, 86
  Mediterranean Fish Casserole, 43
  Mussels Gratinée, 44
  Stuffed Cabbage Leaves with Dill Seeds, 77
Smoked Mackerel Fillets with Smoked Cod's Roe Sauce, 21
Smoked Mackerel Quiche, 46
Souffléed Fish Pie, 45
SORREL
  Chilled Spinach Soup with Almonds, 12
  Tomato and Sorrel Soup with Lovage, 17
SOUP
  Chilled Spinach Soup with Almonds, 12
  Cold (or hot) Curried Fish Soup, 14
  Halibut Soup with Pernod, 12
  Mushroom and Mustard Soup, 15
  Nettle Soup, 16
  Swede and Carrot Soup, 13
  Tomato and Sorrel Soup with Lovage, 17
  Turnip and Spring Onion Soup, 15
Special Shepherd's Pie, 64
Special Terrine of Rabbit with Prunes, 34–35
Special Tomato Salad, 93
Spiced Cheese Straws, 131
Spiced Sesame Fish Bites, 23
SPINACH
  Chilled Spinach Soup with Almonds, 12
  Oriental Pie, 65
  Primrose Salad, 92
  Spinach Wrapped Fish Fillets in Pastry Parcels, 41
SQUID
  Deep Sea Tart, 22
  Mediterranean Fish Casserole, 43
  Noodles with Seafood and Garlic Sauce, 40
  Squid and Tomato Paella, 135
STEAK
  Braised Steak in Sherry with Mushrooms, 56
STRAWBERRY
  Crunchy Layered Strawberry Tart, 104
  Strawberry or Raspberry Cheescake, 107
  Summer Fruit on Yoghurt and Whipped Cream with Hard Sugar Top, 99
Stripy Fish Fillets in Lemon Dressing, 20
Stuffed Boned Chicken en Croûte, 68
Stuffed Cabbage Leaves with Dill Seeds, 77
Stuffed Fillets of Plaice, 45
Stuffed Veal in a Pastry Case, 67
Summer Fruit on Yoghurt and Whipped Cream with Hard Sugar Top, 99
Summer Loaf, 101
Surprise Custard Marrows, 26
SWEDE
  Oriental Pie, 65
  Root Vegetables with Cream and Watercress, 91
  Swede and Carrot Soup, 13
SYLLABUB
  Balkan Syllabub, 120

TAPIOCA
  Old fashioned Nursery Delight, 117
Tarragon Dressing for a Lettuce Salad, 95
TERRINE
  Special Terrine of Rabbit with Prunes, 34–5
TOMATOES
  Baked Spiced Fish, 137
  Calves' Liver with Gooseberry Sauce, 86
  Hearty Beef Casserole, 57
  Hoenyed Pork with Raisins, 50
  Joints of Chicken Baked with Cinnamon, 60
  Kidney Layer Pie, 71
  Kipper and Tomato Soup, 13
  Lanzarote Cassoulet, 136
  Maria's Fish Albongdigas with Devilled Tomato Sauce, 138
  Mediterranean Fish Casserole, 43
  Pigeon Pie, 70
  Putney Pancake Parcel, 75
  Ratatouille in a Veal Case, 66
  Rich Glazed Joint of Brisket, 48
  Roast Juniper Veal and Special Tomato Sauce, 49
  Roast Pheasants with Curried Mushroom Sauce, 53
  Special Shepherd's Pie, 64
  Special Tomato Salad, 93
  Squid and Tomato Paella, 135
  Stuffed Cabbage Leaves with Dill Seeds, 77
  Surprise Custard Marrows, 26
  Sweetbread Risotto, 84
  Tomatoes and Potatoes with Cream and Garlic, 90
  Tomato and Sorrel Soup with Lovage, 17
TREACLE: BLACK
  Cheating Ice Cream with Hot Rum Sauce, 117
  Cold Spiced Ham Baked in Black Treacle, 87
  Rum and Treacle Fruit Cake, 130
Tropical Fruit Salad, 99
Turmeric Pies, 24
TURNIP
  Root Vegetables with Cream and Watercress, 91
  Turnip and Spring Onion Soup, 15
VEAL
  Ratatouille in a Veal Case, 66
  Roast Juniper Veal and Special Tomato Sauce, 49
  Special Terrine of Rabbit with Prunes, 34–5
  Stuffed Veal in a Pastry Case, 67
  Veal Slices with Sage and Parsley, 76
VEGETABLES
  Brussels Sprouts with Almonds and Nutmeg Cream, 91
  Really Good Roast Potatoes, 90
  Root Vegetables with Cream and Watercress, 91
  Tomatoes and Potatoes with Cream and Garlic, 90
WATERCRESS
  Carrot, Hazelnut and Watercress Salad, 93
  Root Vegetables with Cream and Watercress, 91
Water Melon Salad, 92
WINE: RED
  Fillets of Cod in Rich Beetroot Sauce, 42
  Hearty Beef Casserole, 57
  Pigeon Pie, 70
  Rich Glazed Joint of Brisket, 48
  Roast Juniper Veal and Special Tomato Sauce, 49
WINE: WHITE
  Baked Spiced Fish, 137
  Breasts of Chicken Stuffed with Smoked Fish in Mushroom and Prawn Sauce, 80
  Joints of Chicken Baked with Cinnamon, 60
  Lanzarote Cassoulet, 136
  Stuffed Boned Chicken en Croûte, 68
YOGHURT
  Balkan Syllabub, 120
  Blackcurrant Marble Mousse on a Crust, 122
  Creamy Rice with Peaches, 119

YOGHURT – contd.
Crunchy Layered Strawberry Tart, 104
Quick Curried Sauce for Cold Chicken or Turkey, 88
Rose Petal Tart, 105
Summer Fruit on Yoghurt and Whipped Cream with Hard Sugar Top, 99
Tumeric Pies, 24

HERBS AND SPICES

ALLSPICE
Cold Spiced Ham baked in Black Treacle, 87; Hearty Beef Casserole, 57; Rich Glazed Joint of Brisket, 48; Special Terrine of Rabbit with Prunes, 34–5

ANGELICA
Cheese Apples, 115

BASIL
Goats' Cheese Salad with Garbonzas, 134; Putney Pancake Parcel, 75; Special Tomato Salad, 93; Surprise Custard Marrows, 26

BAY
Special Terrine of Rabbit with Prunes, 34–5

CARAWAY
Pork Seed Cakes, 77

CARDAMOM
Apricot Apples Baked with Rum, 103; Autumn Pie with Almond Crust, 110; Cold Stuffed Red Peppers à l'Indienne, 29; Hearty Beef Casserole, 57; Roast Leg of Lamb with Cardamom Sauce, 51; Roast Pheasants with Curried Mushroom Sauce, 53; Spiced Sesame Fish Bites, 23

CHILLI
Almond and Onion Chilli Puff, 33; Devilled Pork Balls with Broad Beans, 28; Maria's Fish Albondigas with Devilled Tomato Sauce, 138; Turmeric Pies, 24

CHIVES
Breasts of Chicken Stuffed with Smoked Fish in a Mushroom and Prawn Sauce, 80; Macaroni in Mayonnaise, 94; Stripy Fish Fillets in Lemon Dressing, 20

CINNAMON
Autumn Pie with Almond Crust, 110; Brandy Spice Ice Cream with Hot Cranberry Sauce, 118; Cashew Nut Fruit Pie, 109; Joints of Chicken Baked with Cinnamon, 60

CORIANDER
Chicken Coriander Pie with Cider and Mustard, 69; Devilled Pork Balls with Broad Beans, 28; Dittisham Casserole, 59; Hearty Beef Casserole, 57; Pigeon Pie, 70; Roast Pheasants with Curried Mushroom Sauce, 53; Spiced Sesame Fish Bites, 23

CUMIN
Almond and Onion Chilli Puff, 33; Baked Spiced Fish, 137; Cold Stuffed Red Peppers à l'indienne, 29; Devilled Pork Balls with Broad Beans, 28; Lamb Fillets with Mint, 59; Marinated Lamb Fillets with Cumin, 78; Meat Loaf with Pumpkin, 74; Roast Pheasants with Curried Mushroom Sauce, 53; Special Shepherd's Pie, 64; Spiced Sesame Fish Bites, 23

CURRY
Baked Spiced Fish, 137; Cold Stuffed Red Peppers à l'Indienne, 29; Curried Baskets Filled with Mushrooms in Mayonnaise, 25; Curried Egg Loaf, 30; Eggs and Onion in Curried Cream Cheese Sauce, 31; Oriental Pie, 65; Quick Curried Sauce for Cold Chicken or Turkey, 88

DILL
Chilled Spinach Soup with Almonds, 12; Curried Baskets filled with Mushrooms in Mayonnaise, 25; Souffléed Fish Pie, 45; Stuffed Cabbage Leaves with Dill Seeds, 77

FENNEL
Breasts of Chicken Stuffed with Smoked Fish in a Mushroom and Prawn Sauce, 80; Halibut Soup with Pernod, 12; Scallops and Prawns in Garlic Cheese Sauce with Sesame Top, 39

GARLIC
Avocados with Cockles and Mussels, 27; Baked Spiced Fish, 137; Braised Steak in Sherry with Mushrooms, 56; Breasts of Chicken Stuffed with Smoked Fish in a Mushroom and Prawn Sauce, 80; Chicken and Nutmeg Lasagne, 82; Chicken Breasts and Almonds in Creamy Cheese Sauce, 81; Cold Stuffed Red Peppers à l'Indienne, 29; Deep Sea Tart, 22; Eggs with Almond and Spring Onion Stuffing, 32; Joints of Chicken Baked with Cinnamon, 60; Kidney Layer Pie, 71; Kipper and Tomato Soup, 13; Kipper Pâté, 35; Lanzerote Cassoulet, 136; Mediterranean Fish Casserole, 43; Mushrooms and Mint, 26; Mussels Gratinée, 44; Noodles with Seafood and Garlic Sauce, 40; Putney Pancake Parcel, 75; Ratatouille in a Veal Case, 66; Roast Juniper Veal and Special Tomato Sauce, 49; Roast Saddle of Lamb with Southern Herb Sauce, 52; Scallops and Prawns in Garlic Cheese Sauce with Sesame Top, 39; Spiced Sesame Fish Bites, 23; Squid and Tomato Paella, 135; Stuffed Boned Chicken en Croûte, 68; Stuffed Veal in a Pastry Case, 67; Swede and Carrot Soup, 13; Tomato and Sorrel Soup with Lovage, 17; Turmeric Pies, 24; Veal Slices with Sage and Parsley, 76

GROUND GINGER
Fillets of Cod in Rich Beetroot Sauce, 42; Roast Pheasants with Curried Mushroom Sauce, 53; Spiced Sesame Fish Bites, 23

JUNIPER
Cold Spiced Ham Baked in Black Treacle, 87; Creamy Blanquette of Rabbit with Mustard, 61; Hearty Beef Casserole, 57; Rich Glazed Joint of Brisket, 48; Roast Juniper Veal and Special Tomato Sauce, 49; Special Terrine of Rabbit with Prunes, 34–5

LOVAGE
Tomato and Sorrel Soup with Lovage, 17

MACE
Apple with Spiced Meringue, 102; Brandy Spice Ice Cream with Hot Cranberry Sauce, 118; Deep Sea Tart, 22; Rich Glazed Joint of Brisket, 48; Rum and Treacle Fruit Cake, 130; Special Terrine of Rabbit with Prunes, 34–5

MARJORAM
Eggs with Almond and Spring Onion Stuffing, 32; Mediterranean Fish Casserole, 43; Stuffed Cabbage Leaves with Dill Seeds, 77

MINT
Almond and Onion Chilli Puff, 33; Calves' Liver with Gooseberry Sauce, 86; Devilled Pork Balls with Broad Beans, 28; Lamb Fillets with Mint, 59; Mushrooms and Mint, 26

NUTMEG
Brussels Sprouts with Almonds and Nutmeg Cream, 91; Chicken and Nutmeg Lasagne, 82; Maria's Fish Albondigas with Devilled Tomato Sauce, 138; Putney Pancake Parcel, 75; Root Vegetables with Cream and Watercress, 91

OREGANO
Chicken Breasts and Almonds in Creamy Cheese Sauce, 81; Kidney Layer Pie, 71; Lanzarote Cassoulet, 136; Pigeon Pie, 70; Putney Pancake Parcel, 75; Roast Saddle of Lamb with Southern Herb Sauce, 52; Sautéed Kidneys in Brandy and Orange Sauce, 85; Special Terrine of Rabbit with Prunes, 34–5; Squid and Tomato Paella, 135; Stuffed Cabbage Leaves with Dill Seeds, 77; Stuffed Fillets of Plaice, 45; Sweetbread Risotto, 84

PAPRIKA
Cheese Apples, 115; Water Melon Salad, 92

PARSLEY
Almond and Onion Chilli Puff, 33; Avocados with Cockles and Mussels, 27; Eggs with Almond and Spring Onion Stuffing, 32; Fillets of Cod in Rich Beetroot Sauce, 42; Mussels Gratinée, 44; Sautéed Kidneys in Brandy and Orange Sauce, 85; Smoked Mackerel Fillets with Smoked Cod's Roe Sauce, 21; Spiced Sesame Fish Bites, 23; Veal Slices with Sage and Parsley, 76

ROSEMARY
Dittisham Casserole, 59; Honeyed Pork with Raisins, 50; Ratatouille in a Veal Case, 66; Rose and Rosemary Junket, 115

SAFFRON
Maria's Fish Albondigas with Devilled Tomato Sauce, 138; Mediterranean Fish Casserole, 43; Squid and Tomato Paella, 135; Sweetbread Risotto, 84

SAGE
Braised Steak in Sherry with Mushrooms, 56; Special Terrine of Rabbit with Prunes, 34–5; Stuffed Veal in a Pastry Case, 67; Veal Slices with Sage and Parsley, 76

SESAME
Oriental Pie, 65; Scallops and Prawns in Garlic Cheese Sauce with Sesame Top, 39; Spiced Sesame Fish Bites, 23

SORREL
Chilled Spinach Soup with Almonds, 12; Tomato and Sorrel Soup with Lovage, 17

TARRAGON
Mackerel en Papillote with Tarragon and Caper Sauce, 38; Stuffed Boned Chicken en Croûte, 68

THYME
Meat Loaf with Pumpkins, 74; Roast Saddle of Lamb with Southern Herb Sauce, 52

TURMERIC
Almond and Onion Chilli Puff, 33; Cold Stuffed Red Peppers à l'Indienne, 29; Mussels Gratinée, 44; Roast Pheasants with Curried Mushroom Sauce, 53; Scallops and Prawns in Garlic Cheese Sauce with Sesame Top, 39; Turmeric Pies, 24